C0-APX-018

The Substitute's Own Survival Guide

by

Dr. Phyllis J. Perry

Publisher

Carson-Dellosa Publishing Company, Inc.

Greensboro, North Carolina

Credits:

Author: Phyllis J. Perry
Project Director: Sherrill B. Flora
Cover illustration: Tim Foley
Inside page illustrations: Vanessa Shwab
Cover Design: Annette Hollister-Papp
Editors: Sherrill B. Flora, Sharon Thompson
Layout Design: Sharon Thompson, Mark Conrad

With deep appreciation to Celeste Woodley for her valuable advice.

Copyright © 2003, Carson-Dellosa Publishing Company, Inc., Greensboro, North Carolina 27425, publishers of the "Stick Out Your Neck" series. All rights reserved. The purchase of this material entitles the buyer to reproduce worksheets and activities for home or classroom use only—not for commercial resale. Reproduction of these materials for an entire school or district is prohibited. No part of this book may be reproduced (except as noted above), stored in a retrieval system, or transmitted in any form or by any means (mechanically, electronically, recording, etc.) without the prior written consent of Carson-Dellosa Publishing Co., Inc.

All rights reserved. Printed in the USA

ISBN:0-88724-964-7

Table of Contents

4-5 Science

4-5 Social Studies

Introduction

Being a substitute teacher is not easy. It demands being resourceful, adaptable, and quick on your feet. A well-developed sense of humor doesn't hurt either! Having *The Substitute's Own Survival Guide* in hand makes substituting a snap! Its quick activities require little or no preparation time and few special materials.

Most teachers leave "plans" to guide the person who comes in to substitute and take over their classes. But even the best laid plans sometimes hit a snag. The film or video that the substitute teacher was supposed to show mysteriously disappears. The librarian must cancel a story hour because she has laryngitis. The eagerly anticipated science guest speaker is involved in a traffic accident and can't visit after all. A fire drill is called and reduces the time available so that the scheduled lesson won't fit into the time that is left.

Sometimes the substitute finds plans for one or two days, but instead of a quick recovery, the patient gets worse and ends up being out for a week. When this happens, the substitute teacher has at least met the students and has some notion of the daily routine, but there is still the question of what to teach.

This book contains activities in language arts, math, science, and social studies. They require few materials and little preparation time; they are fun; they are challenging; and, they may just make the difference in changing a stressful day into a successful one. Although designed for the substitute teacher, these lessons are equally appropriate for the general classroom teacher, especially for use on one of those days when some aspect of the well-planned school day goes awry.

The activities have been suggested as appropriate for certain grade levels, but an educator may certainly adjust the lessons up or down to fit the needs of students. The lessons are presented as discrete activities, but some could easily fit together in a cohesive unit. All can be expanded and modified in the hands of creative teachers.

Teaching in the twenty-first century requires familiarity not only with students and local and state curriculum, but also with national standards. These standards will be touched upon only briefly here, but the activities that follow have been designed to help meet the standards in language arts, math, science, and social studies.

A symbol (or in some cases more than one) in the upper right-hand corner of each page identifies which of the core subject areas is being emphasized in the activity. A pen and paper signifies language arts; a ruler signifies math; a microscope signifies science; and a globe signifies social studies. Beneath the icon, a word or short phrase pin-points which goal within the broad discipline is being addressed. This is expanded upon below.

Language Arts Standards

The standards for English and Language Arts were developed by the National Council of Teachers of English (NCTE) and the International Reading Association (IRA). They are based on the belief that all students must have the opportunities and resources to develop needed language skills to pursue life goals and to be productive members of society. The twelve standards, though presented separately, are interrelated and should be considered as a whole.

The NCTE and IRA standards are listed below. The short phrases in italics after each goal indicate the word or phrase that appears in the upper right-hand corner of each page in this book to show the goal emphasis of the activity.

1. Students read a wide range of print and nonprint texts including fiction, nonfiction, classic, and contemporary works; (*wide range of texts*)

2. Students read from many periods and genre; (*different genre*)

3. Students apply a wide range of strategies to comprehend, interpret, and evaluate texts; (*varied strategies*)

4. Students learn to communicate effectively for different purposes with a wide variety of audiences; (*communicate effectively*)

5. Students learn to use different writing process elements to communicate with audiences; (*different writing process elements*)

6. Students learn about language structure and conventions (spelling and punctuation) to create and discuss print and nonprint texts; (*structure and conventions*)

7. Students gather, evaluate, and synthesize data from a variety of sources to communicate their discoveries; (*synthesize data*)

8. Students learn to use a variety of technological and information resources; (*information resources*)

9. Students respect diversity in language use patterns and dialects across cultures, ethnic groups, geographic regions, and social roles; (*diversity*)

10. Students whose first language is not English use their first language to develop competence in English; (*ESL*)

11. Students participate as knowledgeable members of literacy communities; (*literacy communities*)

12. Students use spoken, written, and visual language to accomplish their own purposes. (*accomplish purposes*)

Math Standards

In 1989 a variety of committees of the National Council of Teachers of Mathematics (NCTM) put into use a group of math standards. Committees of educators continued to work to improve these standards, and in the spring of 2000, NCTM published *Principles and Standards for School Mathematics.*

The six principles, five content standards, and five process standards underlie the suggested activities in mathematics in this book. These standards are broadly organized into the groups listed below. These are the words or phrases listed in the upper right-hand corner of each page to show the specific standard being emphasized in the activity.

- Number and Operations
- Problem Solving
- Algebra
- Reasoning and Proof
- Geometry

- Communication
- Measurement
- Connections
- Data Analysis and Probability
- Representation

Science Standards

The National Science Education Standards have been grouped in eight categories. These are listed below and are the words and phrases that are listed in the upper right-hand corner of each page in this book to show the goal emphasis of the activity.

- Unifying Concepts & Processes
- Science as Inquiry
- Physical Science
- Life Science
- Earth and Space Science
- Science and Technology
- Science in Personal and Social Perspective
- History and Nature in Science

Social Studies Standards

The National Council for Social Studies identified eleven thematic strands that form the basis of the social studies standards. These strands are as follows and are the phrases used in the upper right-hand corner of each page to indicate the goal emphasis of the activity.

- Citizenship
- Culture
- Time
- Continuity and Change
- Space and Place
- Individual Development and Identity
- Individuals, Groups and Institutions
- Production, Distribution and Consumption
- Power, Authority, and Governance
- Science, Technology and Society
- Global Connections

These themes draw from the social studies disciplines of anthropology, economics, geography, history, law, political science, psychology, and sociology. Each grade level builds on the performance expectations from the preceding grades. In general, the social studies curriculum moves from the individual and family outward to neighborhood, communities, regions of the United States and its history and geography, and finally to world regions, geography, and history.

A substitute teacher would be wise to collect a few items in a briefcase, tote bag, or box and carry this collection when sent out on assignment. Included among these treasures might be *The Substitute's Own Survival Guide,* a favorite story book, magazines from which to cut pictures, a few back issues of newspapers, a roll of masking tape, some colored markers, colorful post cards, a couple balloons, scissors, a plastic drinking cup, an empty coffee can, an empty soda bottle, a spool of thread, a ball of string, and a ruler. Add more items to this collection as the school year progresses!

Good luck and good teaching!

Billy Goats Gruff

Grade Level: K–1

Approximate Time Required: 10–20 minutes

Purpose: To provide experience in hearing and dramatizing a fairy tale as an example of the fantasy genre.

Materials: a copy of "The Three Billy Goats Gruff."

Directions: Read "The Three Billy Goats Gruff" below (or from a collection of fairy tales).

The Three Billy Goats Gruff

Once upon a time, long, long ago, there lived three brothers who were called the Billy Goats Gruff. Their names were Great Big Billy Goat Gruff, Big Billy Goat Gruff, and Little Tiny Billy Goat Gruff.

They lived in a field near a stream that had a bridge over it. The three billy goats spent their days eating lush green grass. It was quiet and peaceful except when someone tried to cross the bridge.

Whenever that happened, there was first a loud tramp, tramp, tramp of footsteps on the bridge. This always woke up the mean troll who slept under the bridge. And the troll would come up, demand to know who was crossing his bridge, and then would knock whoever it was right into the water.

One day while the three billy goats were eating, Great Big Billy Goat Gruff raised his head and said, "The grass looks greener on the other side of the bridge. I think we should all go over there to eat."

"Good idea," said Big Billy Goat Gruff.

"I'll go first," said Little Tiny Billy Goat Gruff.

Little Tiny Billy Goat Gruff walked onto the bridge. Tramp, tramp, tramp. Out came the troll. "Who's that tramping on my bridge?"

"It's Little Tiny Billy Goat Gruff," the goat answered in a little, tiny voice.

"I'm going to knock you right into the water," said the troll.

"Please," said Little Tiny Billy Goat Gruff, "don't waste your time on me. Wait for my brother. He's right behind me, and he's much bigger than I."

So the troll let Little Tiny Billy Goat Gruff pass over the bridge. Right behind him came Big Billy Goat Gruff. Tramp, tramp, tramp.

Up came the troll, and asked, "Who's that tramping across my bridge?"

"It's Big Billy Goat Gruff," the goat answered, in a big voice.

"I'm going to knock you right into the water."

"Please don't waste your time on me," said Big Billy Goat Gruff. "Wait for my brother. He's right behind me, and he's much bigger than I."

So the troll let Big Billy Goat Gruff pass over the bridge.

Right behind him came Great Big Billy Goat Gruff. Tramp, tramp, tramp.

The troll came up and said, "Who's that tramping across my bridge?"

"It's Great Big Billy Goat Gruff," said the goat in a great big voice.

"I've been waiting for you," said the troll. "I'm going to knock you into the water."

"Just you try," said Great Big Billy Goat Gruff, and he lowered his head and used his horns like a battering ram.

Great Big Billy Goat Gruff knocked the Troll right into the water. The Troll swam away and never bothered anyone again. And after that, the three Billy Goats Gruff ate sweet green grass on whichever side of the bridge they wanted.

(At this point, stop reading and ask for volunteers to play each of the billy goats and the troll, stressing that to prevent anyone from being hurt, the troll and Great Big Billy Goat Gruff must PRETEND to try to knock each other into the water but must not really hit or push. Let the children take their places and act out the story. For sound effects, the whole class may make the "tramp, tramp, tramp" sounds by slapping the tops of their desks or table in unison whenever anyone crosses the bridge. A low table for a bridge with a chair to assist in climbing up or down might be used if it can be safely arranged. A piece of blue cloth might serve as the stream. More than one cast may volunteer to act out the story.)

Three Billy Goats Gruff Patterns

Little Tiny
Billy Goat

Big Billy Goat

Great Big Billy Goat

Three Billy Goats Gruff Patterns

Troll

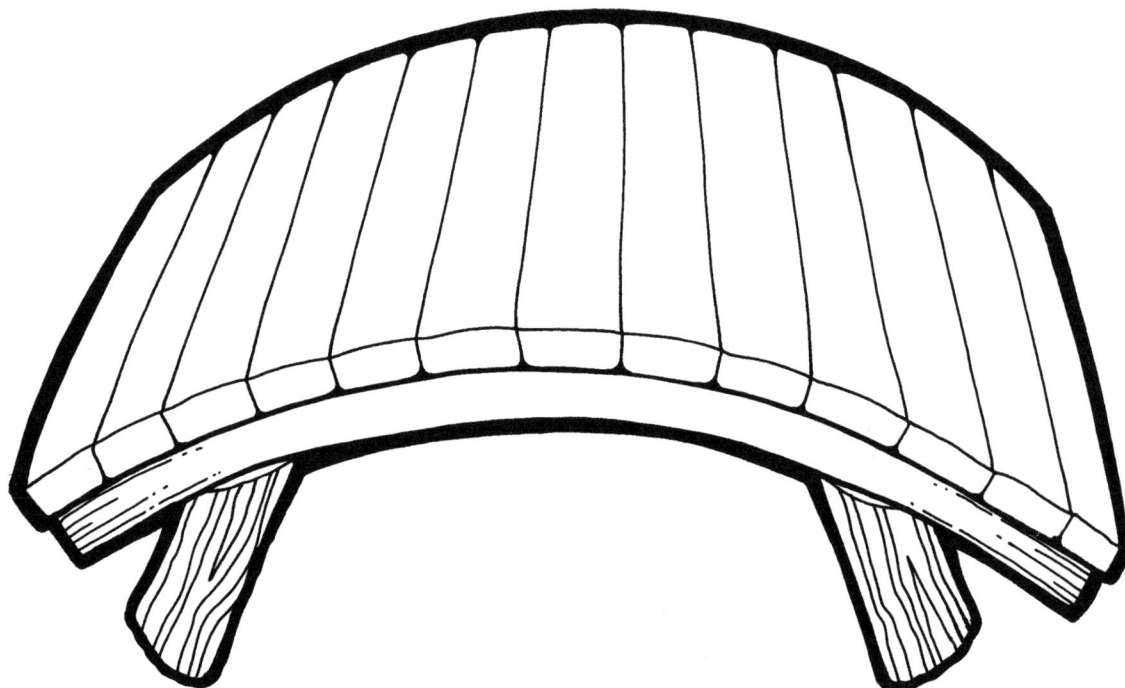

Bridge

Describing Sensory Information

Grade Level: K–1

Approximate Time Required: 15 minutes

Purpose: To provide practice in putting into words the input from sensory data.

Materials: none needed

Directions: Gather students together and remind them that all day long they take in sensory data. They see, hear, smell, taste, and touch many things during the day. The stories that they write or tell are more vivid when they include some of this sensory detail. After each prompt below, pause and allow several volunteers to describe the sensation.

Close your eyes and imagine that you are barefoot and are walking through a squishy mud puddle on a summer day. How does it make you feel?

Suppose you have just tasted the first bite of whipped cream on top of an ice-cream sundae. How does it make you feel?

What if you go to visit Grandma in her apartment, and she has just finished baking chocolate-chip cookies? How does Grandma's kitchen smell, and how does it make you feel?

Imagine that you have gone for a ride on a Ferris wheel at a carnival or amusement park, and the wheel stops at the very top. How does it make you feel?

It's a warm spring day, and it has been raining. The rain stops, and you go outside. What do you see and smell? How does it make you feel?

You drive by a spot in the road where workmen are using a sledge hammer to drill holes in the concrete. What do you hear? What do you see? How does it make you feel?

It's a cold winter day. You are dressed in a coat, hat, gloves, scarf, and boots. You go outside and start to build a snowman. How does your nose feel? How does it feel when you breathe in the frosty air?

Kittens

Grade Level: K–1

Approximate Time Required: 10 minutes

Different Genre

Purpose: To share a simple finger action rhyme with students.

Materials: a stuffed cat toy or cat puppet (optional)
the finger rhyme at the bottom of this page

Directions: If possible, gather the students in a comfortable carpeted section of the room. and have a stuffed cat toy or a puppet to set the scene. If you have a stuffed toy or puppet, ask the students what might be a good name for the kitty. Let volunteers share what they know about kittens. Then tell the students that you are going to recite a finger rhyme about kittens. As you recite the rhyme below, lead the action and encourage the children to go through the motions with you.

Ten Little Kittens

(Hold up both hands with palms facing out.)
Ten little kittens curled in a heap.
(Partly curl all 10 fingers down.)
Every tiny kitten fell fast asleep.
(Close up both hands tightly into fists.)
Five little kittens woke up and stretched.
(Hold up 5 fingers of right hand, spreading the fingers wide)
They ran to the right.
(Move right hand quickly to the right.)
Then they ran to the left.
(Move right hand back to the left.)
The other five kittens came wide awake.
(Hold up 5 fingers of left hand.)
All ten bounced up and down, shouting "Isn't this great?"
(Open and close the fingers of both hands.)
All ten kittens jumped down and started to play.
(Drops both hands down to side and wiggle fingers.)
And they played and played 'til the end of the day!
(Stop wiggling fingers.)

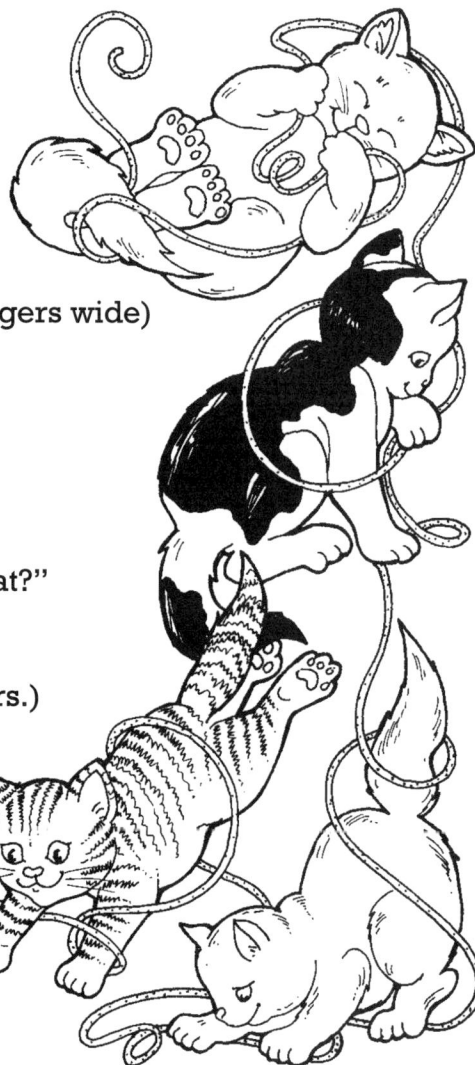

The Gingerbread Man

Grade Level: K-1

Approximate Time Required: 15 minutes

Purpose: To share a traditional folk tale and encourage action to dramatize the story.

Materials: a copy of the story "The Gingerbread Man"
For each student:
a copy of the Gingerbread Man Pattern

Directions: Read the story of "The Gingerbread Man" to the class. You may use the version which appears below, or use a copy of the story from home, school, or public library. As you read the story, ask the children to run in place every time you say, "Run, run, as fast as you can." When you've read the story, have children color their Gingerbread Man.

Once upon a time there lived a little old woman and a little old man. One day the old woman baked a gingerbread cookie. To her surprise, when she opened the oven door, out jumped the gingerbread man, and he ran away! "Wait, wait!" cried the little old woman, but the gingerbread man did not wait. He ran straight down the road. The little old woman and the little old man ran after him. The gingerbread man said,

"Run, run as fast as you can. You can't catch me. I'm the gingerbread man."

The gingerbread man kept running until he came to two men cutting wheat. "Stop!" called one of the men, because he wanted to eat the gingerbread man. The gingerbread man did not stop, so the two men and the little old woman and the little old man all ran after him. "Run, run as fast as you can," the gingerbread man said. "You can't catch me. I'm the gingerbread man."

The gingerbread man ran right past a cow. "Stop!" cried the cow. The cow, the two men, and the little old woman and the little old man ran after him. "Run, run as fast as you can. You can't catch me. I'm the gingerbread man."

Then the gingerbread man ran past a huge pig. "Stop!" called the pig, but the gingerbread man did not stop, and the pig, the cow, the two men, and the little old woman and the little old man ran after him. "Run, run as fast as you can," the gingerbread man called. "You can't catch me. I'm the gingerbread man."

The gingerbread man reached the river. A fox offered to carry him across. The fox started swimming while everyone watched from the shore. When the gingerbread man started to get wet, he climbed right up on the fox's nose. Snap! The fox ate him in one gulp. After all, that's what a gingerbread man is for. "Oh, dear," said the little old woman. I shall have to bake another." And she did.

Gingerbread Man Pattern

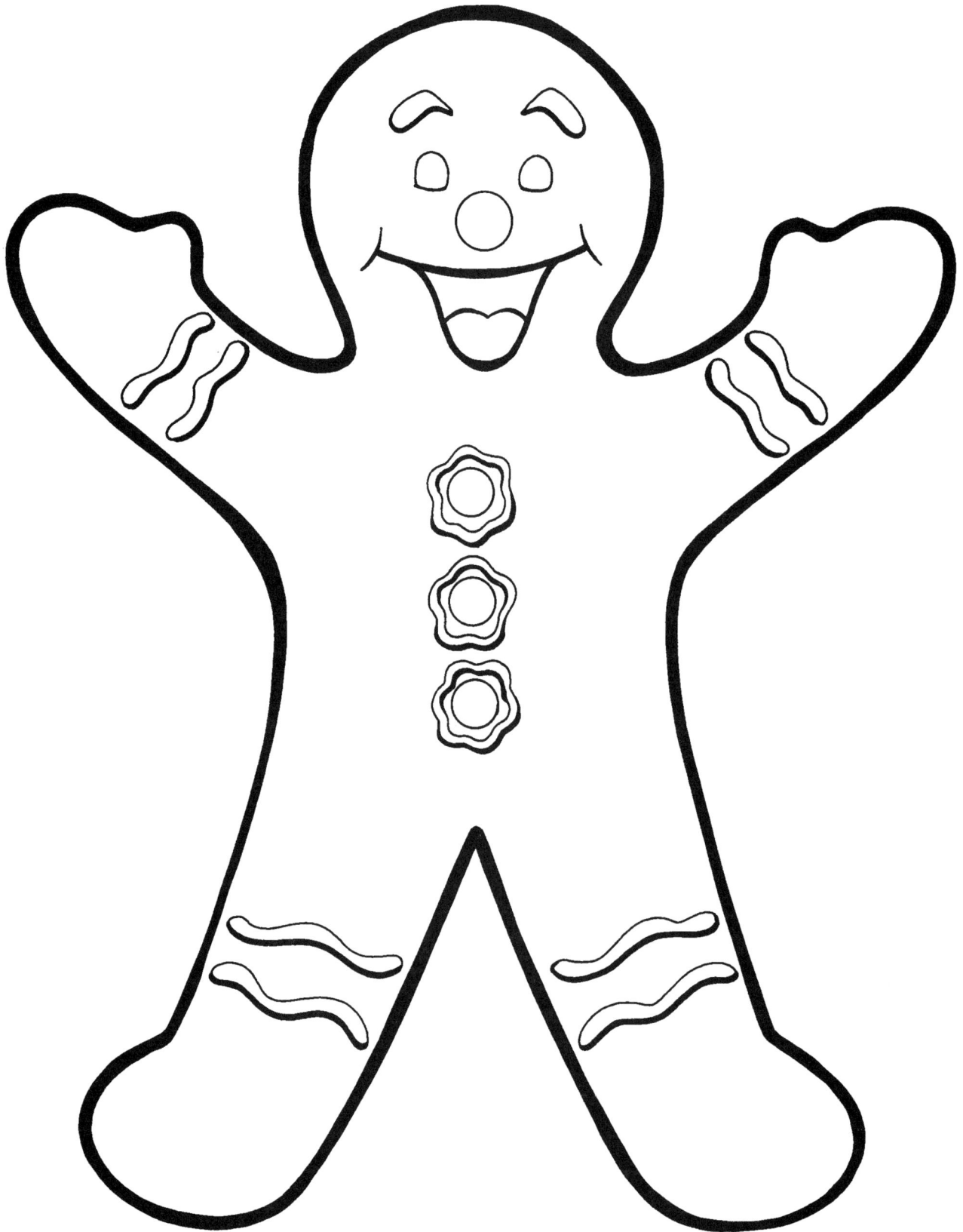

Sequence

Grade Level: K–1

Approximate Time Required: 15 minutes

Varied Strategies

Purpose: To encourage students to correctly sequence the beginning, middle, and ending of a story and to visually represent the story.

Materials: For each student:
a copy of the reproducible on page 18
a sheet of paper
pencil
crayons

Directions: Print the story below on the chalkboard or on the overhead projector. Hand out a copy of the reproducible on page 18 to each student.

Show students the story below written on the overhead projector or chalkboard. Tell them there is a complete story here, with a beginning, a middle, and an ending, but that the sentences are not in the right order. Ask the students to help you decide what comes first, second, third, and fourth in the story.

A tiny green plant grew out of the dirt.
Mary picked a flower and put it in a jar on the table.
Mary and her mother planted a flower seed.
The tiny green plant got big and grew lots of flowers.

Read the story aloud and help the students to decide which sentence should come first to begin the story. Have students put the numeral 1 in the box above this sentence on their copy of page 18. Students should see that the first sentence, or beginning of the story, is "Mary and her mother planted a flower seed."

Continue this process through the other sentences. Students will identify "A tiny green plant grew out of the dirt," and label it #2. Students will identify "The tiny green plant got big and grew lots of flowers," and label it #3. Finally, they will identify the ending as "Mary picked a flower and put it in a jar on the table," and label it #4. Reread the whole story in the right sequence to show that it makes sense.

Have students cut between the illustrations on the dotted lines. They then should paste the illustrations in order on another sheet of paper and color them.

A tiny green plant
grew out of the dirt.

Mary picked a flower and put it
in a jar on the table.

The tiny green plant got big
and grew lots of flowers.

Mary and her mother
planted a flower seed.

© Carson-Dellosa
CD-0048 *The Substitute's Own Survival Guide*

Alphabet Game

Grade Level: K-1

Approximate Time Required: 10 minutes

Purpose: To play a game using beginning sounds.

Materials: a chalkboard eraser

Directions: Ask the students to sit in a circle. Have one child sit in the middle of the circle and close his or her eyes. Give a chalkboard eraser to one student who is sitting somewhere in the circle, and have the students pass the eraser clockwise around the circle.

Whenever the person sitting in the center of the circle wishes, he or she says, "Stop," and looks up, opening his or her eyes. The person holding the eraser at that point stands up. Call out a random letter of the alphabet (being careful not to use the letters q, u, v or x, y, z, since it is harder to think of words beginning with these less common letters). The person standing up then names five words starting with the letter of the alphabet that you called out. For example, if you say "w," the student might say wagon, water, window, Wednesday, and wiggle.

If the student can name five words, he or she goes and sits in the center of the circle. If the student cannot name five words in a reasonable length of time, or if the student names incorrect words, you and the rest of the students may "help." You may help by suggesting other words until the student has met with success and named five words starting with that letter of the alphabet.

The student who was standing goes and sits in the center of the circle, and the student who was sitting in the center comes out and joins in the circle.

Then the game starts over with the passing of the eraser around the circle until the student in the middle calls, "Stop!" and opens his or her eyes and looks up. The child holding the eraser at that point stands up. Call out another letter of the alphabet, and the student who is standing tries to name five words that start with that letter.

Family Puppet Show

Grade Level: K–1

Approximate Time Required: 15 minutes

Purpose: To create simple family puppets and plays.

Materials:

For each student::
a facial tissue
4 cotton balls
a small rubber band

For each table:
a box of markers

Accomplish Purposes

Directions: Divide the class into groups with four or five students at each table. Explain that you will show students how to make simple puppets. Each student's puppet needs to be a family member: a father, mother, grandfather, grandmother, aunt, uncle, brother, or sister.

Demonstrate each step in the puppet-making process. First take a tissue and put it flat on the table in front of you. Put four to five cotton balls in the center of the tissue. Pick up the tissue, holding the cotton balls close together in one hand. Use the other hand to slip a small rubber band over the cotton balls to act as a "neck," holding the cotton balls in the head of the puppet.

Explain that each table of students is to plan a short puppet show in which a family has dinner, goes for a ride in a car, celebrates a birthday, goes for a picnic in a park, or does some other simple activity. Decide who will play the part of father, grandfather, uncle, or son. Who will play the part of mother, grandmother, aunt, or daughter? What activity will they do? What words will each family member say? Will they be happy, sad, excited, or angry?

Use the markers to draw faces and hair on the puppet heads. Put on eyes, a nose, a mouth, and a little colored hair. When the puppets are finished, each student puts a puppet over his or her hand with the index finger up through the rubber band into the head of the puppet. Let each table practice acting out a family puppet show.

If there is time, each table of students may present their family puppet show to the whole class.

How Many?

Grade Level: K–1

Approximate Time Required: 15 minutes

Purpose: To provide experience in computing, using objects.

Number and Operation

Materials: **For each team of students:**

a box or can of objects including:
tens sticks
buttons
clothespins
paper clips
other small objects

Directions: Divide the class into six teams. Tell students that they are going to listen to some problems and try to solve them. Stress that it is important to listen very carefully to the problem before they begin working. After they have heard the problem, the team members are to work together to solve the problem. They can use the objects that you put on each table (tens sticks, buttons, clothespins, paper clips, etc.) to help them solve the problem. When the team members agree that they have the answer, they raise their hands.

After most teams have solved each problem, call on the teams to explain to the rest of the class how they went above solving the problem.

1. A class of students is going on a field trip. Instead of going on a bus, they are going to go in cars. Each parent or teacher that volunteers to drive on the trip may take up to four students. If there are twenty-two students in the class, how many cars are needed for the trip? (Volunteer to read the problems aloud more than once.)

2. The class is going to have cookies at a party. There are twenty-four students in the class. If each student is going to get to eat three cookies at the party, how many cookies do they need?

3. Grandma wanted to know how many picture books Mary read during the week. Mary counted and wrote down the number of books she read each day. On Sunday, she read four books. On Monday, she read two books. On Tuesday she read three books. On Wednesday, she read one book. On Thursday, she read four books. On Friday she read two books. And on Saturday she read five books. In all, how many books did Mary read that week?

How Wide Is the Door?

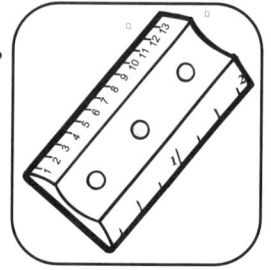

Grade Level: K–1

Approximate Time Required: 15 minutes

Measurement

Purpose: To provide experience in exploring measurement.

Materials: scissors
ball of yarn or string
For each team:
Five common classroom objects such as:
unsharpened pencils
large paper clips
small paper clips
boxes of chalk
stacks of 3" x 5" index cards
chalkboard
chalk

For each student:
a copy of Fun Rulers on page 23

Directions: Gather students around and ask them how they might measure the width of the classroom door and listen to their suggestions. Some may suggest using a ruler, a yard stick, a meter stick, or a tape measure to do the measurement. Others may suggest nonstandard measurements. Go to the door with two students and ask them to measure off the width of the door, using a piece of string or yarn. Help one student hold one end of the string or yarn at the edge of the door while the other brings the string or yarn straight across the door to the other side. Then cut the string or yarn so that it is the same width as the door. Using this piece as a model, cut other lengths of string so that there are five pieces of string or yarn that are the same length and that are the same width as the door.

Divide the class into five teams naming them Team A, B, C, D, or E. Each team will work in a different section of the room. Team members are to stretch out their piece of string or yarn on a table or on the floor and then "measure it." They are to find out how wide the door is in pencils, pieces of chalk, small and large paper clips, and index cards. Point out that the measurements may not come out evenly. The string (or door width) may be 8½ cards wide, or 24½ small paper clips wide.

When the team has a measurement, one team member reports it to you, and you record it on the chalkboard. Write A, B, C, D, and E along the top of the chalkboard. Down the side write pencils, chalk, small paper clips, large paper clips, index cards. When a team reports a number, record it on the chalkboard in the correct place on the graph. When all measurements are complete, gather students around the chalkboard to see how close they agree in their measurements. The discussion should create an awareness that standard measurements and measurement tools are helpful and that different measuring tools may give different numerical measurements of the same object.

Have students cut out the rulers from page 23 and measure different items with them. For example, a student's desk may be nine cats wide.

Fun Rulers

5   4   3   2   1

7   6   5   4   3   2   1

6   5   4   3   2   1

Ice-Cream Flavors

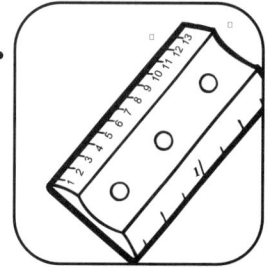

Grade Level: K–1

Approximate Time Required: 10–20 minutes

Purpose: To provide experience in collecting and representing data in a graph.

Materials:
chalkboard
yardstick
pink, brown, orange, and white chalk
48 squares of 3" x 3" construction paper:
12 each in pink, brown, orange, and white
masking tape

Directions: Prepare a graph ahead of time. Draw it with chalk on the chalkboard, using a yardstick. Along the horizontal axis, write strawberry (using pink chalk), vanilla (using white chalk), chocolate (using brown chalk), and orange sherbet (using orange chalk). Along the vertical axis, list numbers 1 to 15. At the top, write "Our Favorite Ice-Cream Flavors."

Explain that sometimes in the newspaper or in books students may see a drawing that looks something like this one. Tell them it is called a graph, and it shows information in a way that is easy to understand. You'll make a graph today that shows how the class feels about different flavors of ice cream. You'll find out which is the favorite flavor of ice cream of your class members. There are lots of special flavors, and all of them aren't listed here, but today students will choose their favorite from these four flavors: strawberry, vanilla, chocolate, or orange sherbet. As you list the four flavors, hold up squares of pink, white, brown, and orange paper.

One by one, invite the children to come up, choose a square of pink, white, brown, or orange paper to indicate their favorite flavor of ice cream, and come sit in front of the graph. Have students come up one by one as you place a piece of masking tape (a small circle that will be sticky on both sides) on the back of their piece of construction paper. Then they stick their colored paper square in the right column for strawberry, vanilla, chocolate, or orange sherbet.

When all the squares have been taped in columns on the chalkboard, have students answer questions such as the following: Which is the favorite flavor in this class? How many people in the class picked this as their favorite? Which is the least favorite flavor?

(The same activity can be done by making the graph using markers on a large sheet of chart paper. Then the completed graph could be displayed on a bulletin board.)

Picture Math

Grade Level: K–1

Approximate Time Required: 10–20 minutes

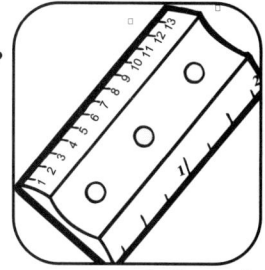

Purpose: To provide experience in using reasoning and problem solving.

Materials: paper and pencils
Math Problems reproducible on page 25

Directions: Hand each student a copy of the reproducible. Read the problems below, asking students to make pictures on their paper to help them solve each problem. As each problem is solved, invite a student to come to the chalkboard and draw a picture showing how he or she solved the problem, telling what the answer is.

1. Two puppies lived on the farm. One puppy had three black spots. The other puppy had five black spots. How many spots in all were there on both puppies?

2. The three children who lived on the farm each owned some ducks. Billy had three ducks. Joanie had two ducks. Tim had five ducks. How many ducks in all did the three children own?

3. Joanie picked some flowers from the garden to take to grandmother. She picked two white flowers, four yellow flowers, and two red flowers. In all, how many flowers did she pick?

4. In the spring, several baby animals were born on the farm. There were eight little pigs. There was one baby horse. There were two baby calves. In all, how many baby animals were born on the farm?

5. Billy gathered eggs from the henhouse. There were ten nests. There was a fresh egg in every nest but one. How many eggs did Billy collect?

6. Tommy picked three pea pods in the garden. One pea pod had three peas in it. One pod had two peas in it. Another pod had five peas in it. How many peas were in all the pods?

Math Problems

1.

2.

3.

4.

5.

6.

Popular Pet

Grade Level: K–1

Approximate Time Required: 10–15 minutes

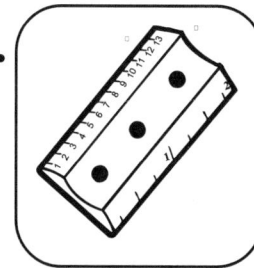

Data Analysis

Purpose: To provide experience in collecting and showing data on a bar graph.

Materials: three containers (bowls, boxes, or coffee cans)
magazine pictures (dog, cat, other small pets)
chalkboard
chalk
counters (seeds, pennies, candies)

Directions: Put three containers (bowls, boxes, or coffee cans) on a table. Put a magazine picture of a dog on one container and a picture of a cat on another container. On the third container put pictures of various animals that are kept as pets such as turtles, gerbils, birds, snakes, and rabbits. Make a large graph on a piece of chart paper or on the chalkboard. Write "cats" (with a picture of a cat) and "dogs" (with a picture of a dog), and "other" (with pictures of birds, rabbits, snake, etc.) along the bottom axis. Along the vertical axis, write the numbers from 1 to 10. Have counters to hand out to each student.

Talk with the class about pets, bringing out the fact that many people, young and old, have pets. Some people in the class, or their relatives or friends, keep pets such as cats, dogs, snakes, gerbils, goldfish, parrots, or rabbits. Some keep more than one pet. Allow time for children to discuss pets that they or their relatives or friends have, or once had, or would like to have.

Tell students that you are going to collect information about popular pets. Each student will be given a counter and can vote for his or her favorite pet, making a choice from a cat, a dog, or some other animal. Explain that a vote for "other" means that the child's most favorite pet could be a goldfish, a bird, a rabbit, a turtle, a gerbil, or some other interesting animal.

When everyone understands the three choices, give each child a counter and let the students come up, one by one, and drop their counter into one of the three containers.

When everyone has had a chance to vote, say that you are going to show the results of the vote for the most popular pet by coloring in your bar graph. Count the number of counters in the cat container, and shade up to that number above cats on the graph. Then count and announce the number of votes for "dogs" and shade up to that number above dogs on the graph. Then count the number of others and shade up to that number of squares above "others" on the graph. Talk about the results. Which kind of pet is the most popular in this class?

Farm and Zoo

Grade Level: K–1

Approximate Time Required: 15–20 minutes

Purpose: To provide experience showing data in a bar graph.

Materials: magazine pictures of various animals
chalkboard
chalk

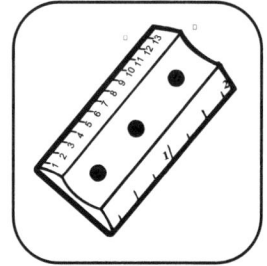

Data Analysis

Directions: Have magazine pictures of various farm and zoo animals to hand out to each student. There should be some singleton pictures and some multiple pictures of the same animals. For example, there may be one zebra and six ducks. On the chalkboard, numerals from 1 to 6 should go up the vertical axis. Along the horizontal axis, write the names of pictured animals such as duck, cow, pig, zebra, elephant, and camel.

Tell the class that they are to pretend that during the night some of the animals on the nearby farm and the zoo have escaped and are wandering around in a park in town. Their job is to help the farmer and the zookeeper round up all their animals again. Mark off a large circle using a piece of string on the floor saying that one section is a corral for "farm animals." Use another circle of string to mark off another section of the room that is a cage for "zoo animals." Choose one volunteer to be the zookeeper and another volunteer to be the farmer.

Invite each child to come up to a table and pick a picture of a farm animal or a zoo animal. (About six kinds of animals should be represented. For some animals there may be only one or two pictures, while for others there may be four or five pictures.) For example, four students may pick up a picture of a rabbit and choose to be rabbits. One child picks up the one picture of the zebra and is the only zebra. Each child is to hold the picture up in front of his or her chest. Once all the students have chosen an animal, they may move around the room until the farmer or zookeeper comes up to them. Then they are to be led quietly to the corral for farm animals or to a cage for zoo animals.

Once all the animals are rounded up, the farmer and the zookeeper count how many animals of each kind they have and mark the graph. The completed graph might show six ducks, two cows, four rabbits, one zebra, three elephants, and five camels. Then ask appropriate questions using the data shown on the graph such as:

How many farm animals were there in all?

How many zoo animals were there in all?

How many more ducks were wandering about than elephants?.

(A similar activity, focusing on ways to classify animals, is given on page 34 and could be combined with this lesson.)

Relative Position

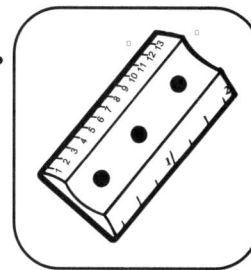

Grade Level: K–1

Approximate Time Required: 10–15 minutes

Geometry

Purpose: To provide experience in locating and describing spatial relationships.

Materials: chalkboard

Directions: Draw on the chalkboard, in order from left to right, a large circle, a small circle, a large square, a small square, a large triangle, and a small triangle. Students should be gathered near the chalkboard. Review the names of the shapes drawn on the chalkboard.

Call one by one for volunteers to come up, take the piece of chalk, and follow the directions read from the list below. (Depending upon the age and skill level of the students involved, you may wish to add or subtract to this suggested list.)

Put an X between the small circle and the large square.
Put an X in the middle of the small square.
Draw a line under the big triangle.
Draw a line over the large circle.
Put an X beneath the small triangle.
Draw a small circle near but not on the small triangle.
Draw one line to divide the large circle in half.
Put an X under the small circle.
Draw a line to divide the small square in half.

After each student carries out one of the above directions, reinforce the correct answers. (Sometimes there can be several correct responses. For example, if a student divides the small square in half using a vertical line, another student might volunteer, "I see another way to divide the square in half," and the student draws a horizontal line. In these cases, point out that both answers are correct.) If the student errs, assist the student in correcting his or her response.

Once students have completed the activity above, have them complete the reproducible Following Directions on page 30.

Following Directions

1. Draw and color a sun.
2. Draw and color a duck on the pond.
3. Draw and color a bird in the sky.
4. Draw and color a dog by the doghouse.
5. Draw and color a cat in the tree.
6. Color the grass green.
7. Draw and color a picture of yourself on the swing.

What's Missing?

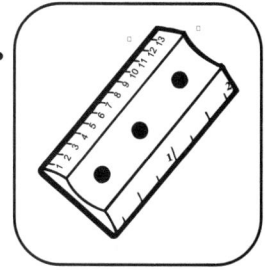

Grade Level: K–1

Approximate Time Required: 10 minutes

Geometry

Purpose: To provide experience in visualization of shapes.

Materials: several small objects
overhead projector and screen

Directions: Tell students that they are going to play a game called "What's missing?".

Tell students that you will project several objects onto the screen and give them time to look at them. Then you will turn off the projector and take away one or two of the objects. When you turn the projector back on again, ask "What's missing?" Students will try to remember which object or objects that were there are gone.

For example, put on the overhead projector small scissors, a paper clip, a rubber band, a block, a pencil, and a quarter. Name each object as it is placed on the overhead projector.

Turn off the projector and take away the rubber band without allowing the students to see it being removed. Then ask "What's missing?" Call on students to give the answer.

Begin by projecting the same five objects each time and by taking away a single object. As students gain in their ability to solve the problem by answering correctly, you may want to remove two objects when you turn off the projector, and you may want to increase the number of objects involved from five to seven or nine.

Alike and Different

Grade Level: K–1

Approximate Time Required: 10–15 minutes

Physical Science

Purpose: To provide experience in discussing things in terms of likenesses and differences.

Materials: For each student:

a copy of the reproducible Venn diagram on page 33

Directions: Gather students together and explain that they are going to use their observation skills and their science thinking skills. Use the questions below to get started, and add others as you go along.

Tell them that they are going to observe some of the things around the room to see how they are alike and how they are different.

How are tables and chairs alike?
How are tables and chairs different?
How are children and plants alike?
How are children and plants different?
How are the ceiling and the floor alike?
How are the ceiling and the floor different?
How are a pencil and a piece of chalk alike?
How are a pencil and a piece of chalk different?

Now we're going to think about some things that aren't in the room and see if we can tell ways they are alike and ways in which they are different.

How are a fish and a guinea pig alike?
How are a fish and a guinea pig different?
How are a tree and a rosebush alike?
How are a tree and a rosebush different?
How are a football and a basketball alike?
How are a football and a basketball different?
How are daffodils and carrots alike?
How are daffodils and carrots different?

Allow time for discussion and for each child to contribute ideas.

Once you've explored all the questions above, choose two topics to compare and contrast. Have students fill in their Venn diagrams.

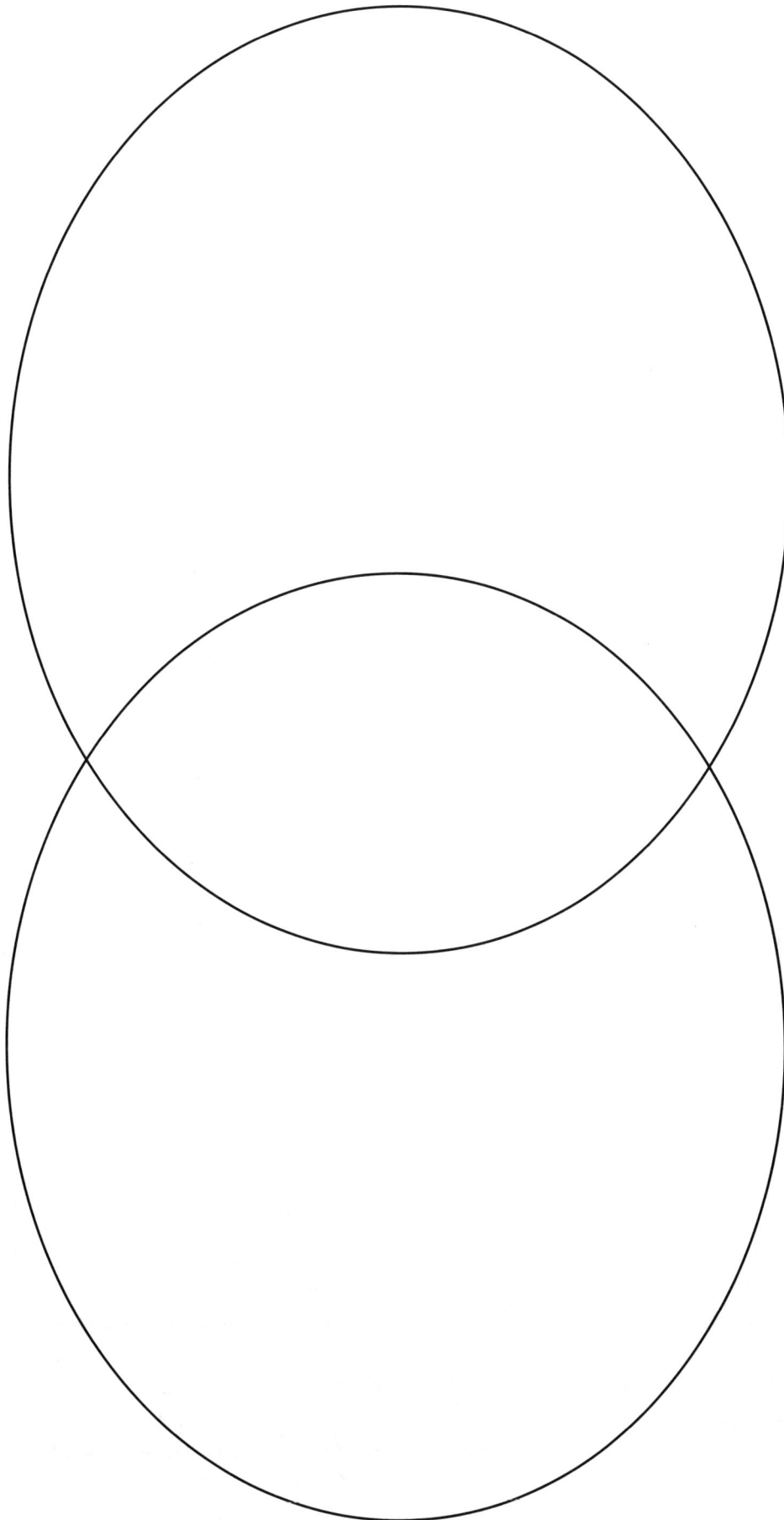

Name

Venn Diagram

Classifying Animals

Grade Level: K–1

Approximate Time Required: 10–20 minutes

Life Science

Purpose: To provide experience in different ways of classifying animals.

Materials: construction paper
magazine pictures or simple drawings of animals

Directions: Prepare ahead of time sheets of construction paper. Each sheet will have printed on it the name of an animal and a picture cut from a magazine or a simple drawing of that animal. Tell students that they are to pretend that during the night all the animals on the nearby farm and the zoo have escaped and are wandering around in a park in town. Their job is to help the farmer and the zookeeper to round up all their animals again.

Choose one child to be the farmer and designate one section of the room as "the farm." Then choose another child to be the zookeeper and designate one section of the room as "the zoo."

A child comes up and picks up one of the sheets of construction paper with the name and picture of an animal on it, and holds it up so all the class can see. Then you should ask, "Should this animal be sent to the farm or the zoo?" The class decides, and the farmer takes the child carrying the card to the farm, or the zookeeper takes the child carrying the card over to the area designated as the zoo.

The cards and pictures prepared ahead of time might show pig, tiger, rooster, giraffe, duck, elephant, cow, kangaroo, horse, rhino, sheep, polar bear, monkey, hen, camel, turkey, lion, goat, hippo, and donkey.

Follow up this discussion with other ways in which animals might be classified.

Children might suggest any of the following or others: animals that can (or can't) fly, animals that spend (or do not spend) most of their lives in water; animals that do (or don't) have fur; animals that do (or don't) spend most of their lives underground; animals that do (or don't) have feathers; animals that do (or don't) have scales; animals that do (or don't) have horns or antlers; animals that do (or don't) lay eggs, animals that do (or don't) have hooves, animals that do (or don't) have legs, etc. When something is suggested as a criteria for classification, take time to suggest one or two animals that fit or don't fit that criteria. (A similar activity in graphing zoo and farm animals as a mathematics skill appears on page 28 and could be combined with this activity.)

Listen to the Pitch

Grade Level: K–1

Approximate Time Required: 15 minutes

Physical Science

Purpose: To demonstrate that different sounds can be made with the same objects if the objects are of the same thickness but different sizes.

Materials: three empty widemouth jars of graduated sizes (with same thickness of glass)
three empty drinking glasses of graduated sizes (with same thickness of glass)
spoon

Directions: Ask a student to arrange the three empty jars on the table from the smallest to the largest. Ask another student to arrange the drinking glasses on the table from smallest to largest.

Ask the children to listen carefully as you strike the smallest jar with a spoon. Then strike the middle jar with a spoon and ask, "Do the two jars make exactly the same sound when I strike them?" (Children may disagree.) Say, "Listen as I strike the two jars again. Which one makes the higher sound?" (Most children will agree the smaller jar makes the higher sound.)

"What sort of sound do you think the biggest jar will make? Will it be the same, sound lower, or sound higher?" Allow students to predict. Strike all three jars, one after another from biggest to smallest. (The sound should get higher each time.) Talk about this. Mention that larger and thicker objects make lower sounds when they vibrate.

Then turn to the three glasses. Ask volunteers to predict which of the glasses will make the highest sound when struck with the spoon and which will make the lowest sound. Then, using the spoon, strike the glasses and discuss whether or not the student predictions were correct.

If other objects are available, you can continue to use other sets of objects to demonstrate pitch differences. (The difference between each of the objects in the set must be fairly great for children to be able to hear the difference in sound. Also the glass in the jars or the drinking glasses must be about the same thickness.)

Healthy Me

Grade Level: K–1

Approximate Time Required: 10–20 minutes

Science in Personal and Social Perspectives

Purpose: To develop students understanding of responsibility for their own health.

Materials: **For each student:**
  copy of Keeping Healthy reproducible on page 37
  pencils
  crayons

Directions: Bring the class together to discuss health issues. You might ask, "What can each of you do in the morning before you come to school that will help keep you healthy?" Responses might include brush my teeth, bathe or wash my hands, eat a good breakfast. Hand out the Keeping Healthy reproducible on page 37 and have each child write his or her name on the blank. Then allow time for each student to draw a picture in the square showing a healthy morning habit.

Next ask what a student might do during the day at school to help all classmates keep healthy. Responses might include follow playground rules to avoid accidents; cover coughs and sneezes so as not to spread germs; keep classroom toys, blocks, etc. out of mouths. Again allow time for each student to draw a picture in the square showing a healthy habit that protects others.

Next, discuss with students what might be done after school to help keep healthy. Responses might be to get exercise; eat a healthy snack and dinner; enjoy some relaxation. Allow time for each student to draw a picture in the squares showing a healthy after-school habit.

Finally, talk about what students might do at bedtime to keep healthy. Responses might include bathe; brush teeth; get plenty of sleep. Allow time for each student to draw a picture in the squares showing a healthy bedtime habit.

If time permits, allow volunteers to share their pictures and tell what healthy habit is being depicted.

Keeping Healthy

In the Morning	**During School**
After School	**At Bedtime**

Sunny Days / Rainy Days

Grade Level: K–1

Approximate Time Required: 15 minutes

Purpose: To provide information about weather fronts.

Earth Science

Materials: construction paper shapes:
sun, daisy, gray cloud, white cloud, sheet of rain drops
For each student:
a copy of Dress for the Weather reproducible on page 39

Directions: Prepare ahead of time some simple weather shapes for the actors to hold during the weather dramatization. Tell students that they are going to study a sunny day and a rainy day. Ask for volunteers to be the sun, a daisy, raindrops, a cold front gray cloud, and a warm front white cloud.

Gather the children into a large circle. Tell students, "Sometimes we have a sunny day." (Ask the child carrying the big picture of the sun to come into the center of the circle.) "On sunny days, it is warm, and often flowers bloom." (Ask the child with the daisy to come into the center of the circle.) "Sometimes, we have a partly cloudy day." (Invite the two children holding white clouds to come into the circle, holding the clouds above their heads.) "These clouds are part of a warm front and contain warm air. Warm air is light. It spreads out and rises."

"Sometimes there is a cold front. During a cold front, a heavy mass of air comes along and sinks." (Invite the two children with gray clouds to come out into the circle, holding their clouds down below their waists.) "On a day like this, it can be very cloudy." Ask the child carrying the sun to sit down.

"When the warm front of air meets the cold front of air, it may begin to rain." (Ask the child carrying the sheet of raindrops to come out into the middle of the circle.)

Collect the sun, daisy, raindrops, and clouds and gather all the students for a weather discussion. Ask what kind of day it is today. Are there any clouds in the sky? What do the clouds look like? Has it been warm or cold? Does anyone know what the high temperature is supposed to be today? Does anyone know how cold it got last night? Allow students to make and share weather observations.

Explain how it is important to dress differently for different types of weather. Have each child complete the reproducible on page 39.

Dress for the Weather

Color the appropriate clothes.

1.

It is cold outside!

2.

It is hot at the beach!

3.

It is raining!

4.

It is a chilly day!

Sorting

Grade Level: K–1

Approximate Time Required: 10–15 minutes

Physical Science

Purpose: To provide experience in showing that objects can be arranged in an orderly way.

Materials: Assorted objects:
  15 assorted buttons
  6 pencils of different sizes
  6 crayons of different sizes and colors
  6 small rocks
  6 small toy cars

Directions: Divide the class into about five groups. Each group may work at a table or on a carpeted section of the floor. Each group will need a box, can, or tray to hold a set of miscellaneous objects. (These objects can be whatever is easily at hand.) Give each group of students a box of miscellaneous materials and have them dump out the contents onto their piece of carpet or their work table.

Say, "In front of you is a messy pile of things. Your job will be to organize the pile in some way. Can you think of a way to group the things into different piles? Work together and see what you can do."

After the students have worked together, discuss how they went about organizing the objects. Perhaps they made piles of buttons, pencils, crayons, rocks, and toy cars.

Now say, "You've done a good job of organizing the big mess into some piles of objects. Now look at each pile. Is there a way you could organize each of the small piles? Talk about it together and then organize the small piles."

Circulate among the groups to see how they are organizing. Some may organize the buttons by size, by number of holes in the button, or by color. Sets can be organized in different ways as long as the objects in the set have one attribute or property in common. The cars could be sorted by "wheels resting on the carpet" or "wheels pointing in the air" or they could be sorted by color. Pencils might be sorted by size. Encourage the students to have many ways to organize the materials.

You might conclude by gathering up the supplies and discussing how other things are organized: paper in the classroom, clothes at home, or books in a library.

Hot or Cold?

Grade Level: K–1

Approximate Time Required: 20 minutes

Physical Science

Purpose: To provide experience using the sense of touch. This activity will help the student to understand the relative nature of temperature.

Materials: a blindfold
a towel for drying hands
three containers of water

Directions: Fill the three containers with water: one with comfortably hot tap water, one with cold tap water, and one with slightly warm tap water. Place the three containers side by side on a table, with the warm water in the middle. Tell students that they are going to try to fool their sense of touch. Explain that the three tubs contain water that is hot, warm, and cold. (BE SURE THAT THE HOT TAP WATER IS NOT TOO HOT. TEST IT YOURSELF BEFORE USING IT ON A STUDENT). Ask for a volunteer. The volunteer stands behind the table, in front of the three tubs, facing the class.

Blindfold the child and guide the student's hand and dip it in the cold water. Ask the child, "how does the water feel?" The student will respond, "cold." Then guide the child's other hand and put it in the tub of comfortably hot tap water. Ask "how does the water feel?" The child will respond, "hot."

Take off the blindfold but continue to have the child keep one hand in the cold tap water and another in the comfortably hot tap water. After just a few minutes, ask the child to put both hands in the slightly warm tap water and ask, how does the water feel? The student should respond that the water feels "cool" to the hand that was in the comfortably hot water, but it feels "warm" to the hand that was in the cold water.

If time permits, let other children try the same experiment. (Remember that the comfortably hot tap water will cool and may need to be replaced with more water from the tap as time passes.)

Put on a Happy Face

Grade Level: K–1

Approximate Time Required: 15 minutes

Purpose: To provide experience in knowing that feelings are associated with people.

Individual Development & Identity

Materials: paper
crayons

Directions: Hold a short discussion with students about feelings, pointing out that our faces often reflect our feelings and that we change our expressions many times during the day, although we still remain the same person.

Ask for a number of volunteers to face the group and put expressions on their faces to show a happy face, a sad face, an angry face, and a surprised face.

Talk about the sorts of situations in class and on the playground that cause us to wear different expressions.

Give each student a sheet of drawing paper. Assist the student in folding their sheet of paper in half. Then have them open up the paper sc it is flat on their desk or table top.

Ask the students to draw an oval in each of the two halves. Demonstrate this by drawing two ovals on the chalkboard.

Then have the students draw in eyes, nose, and mouth to show a happy face.

Demonstrate at the chalkboard by drawing your own happy face and then circulate through the room helping and commenting to students.

Next have the children draw a sad face. Again, demonstrate by drawing a face on the chalkboard.

The children may color in hair and eyes.

Take time to allow volunteers to show their happy and sad faces to their classmates.

Have students complete the All About Me reproducible on page 43 and share it with their classmates.

All About Me

My name is _____.

I am _____ years old.

My favorite color is _____.

My favorite animal is _____.

My best friend is _____.

This is me.

This is my room.

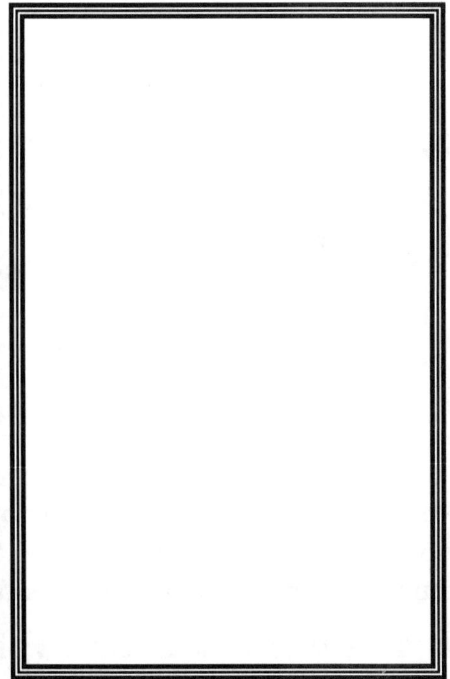

This is my favorite toy.

When I grow up I want to be a

_____.

Assembly Line

Grade Level: K–1

Approximate Time Required: 15 minutes

Purpose: To provide experience in assembling a booklet.

Materials: **For each work station:**
12 pieces of construction paper
18 pieces of plain paper
a stapler and staples

Directions: Divide the class into work groups of six students each. Each work group will sit around a table. In front of the first person is a stack of six sheets of colored construction paper. In front of students #2, #3, #4 are six sheets of plain paper. In front of student #5, is a stack of six sheets of colored construction paper, and in front of student #6 is a stapler.

Tell students that many items that we use every day are not made by a single person but instead are produced in factories where each individual worker has a job to do in a certain order, resulting in a finished product that is then distributed to consumers. Explain that the production line you have set up today will produce books. Demonstrate the process by picking up a piece of colored paper, putting three sheets of lined paper underneath it, adding a piece of construction paper as the back cover and then using a stapler to put in two staples to hold the book together.

Encourage students to be careful as they do their part of the job of making a book. Point out that if the pages are not straight or if the staples are not put in at the edge of the booklet, the booklet will not be as neat as it should be. (You might demonstrate this by making a "neat" book and a "sloppy" book to show the class.)

Then let each team set to work as you circulate around the room, helping each production line to turn out six booklets. (If there are insufficient staplers, or if using the stapler is too difficult, the sixth student at each station can be a "runner" and bring the booklet to be stapled.)

Gather the students together and discuss fun activities they do in "free time." These might be swinging in the park, playing with a dog, reading a book, or baking cookies. Have each student choose one of the booklets that was made by the work team and put his or her name on it. Then ask students to draw three pictures in their booklet, showing what they like to do in their free time.

How Tall?

Measurement

Time, Continuity & Change

Grade Level: K–1

Approximate Time Required: 15 minutes

Purpose: To discuss and measure change over time.

Materials: two sheets of paper
tape measure or yardstick

Directions: Gather students around in a comfortable area for discussion and ask how their families keep records of changes in their children as time goes by. Topics that may come up during this discussion are baby books, scrapbooks, photo albums, etc. You might initiate a discussion about whether anyone records children's heights.

Explain to the class that as children grow, there are many changes. They get new teeth, they get heavier, their hands and feet get bigger, and they get taller. Talk about growth spurts, explaining that a person may not seem to grow much for a long time and then suddenly shoots up all at once.

Explain that today you are going to measure their height using a yardstick or a tape measure, and that you will date the papers and mark each student's height and name on the paper.

Call the students up to the chart one by one. Ask them to take off their shoes and to stand in their stocking feet. Mark off the names and heights of the girls on one sheet of paper, and mark off the names and heights of the boys on another sheet of paper.

If this is near the beginning or middle of the school year, tell the students that you will leave the two sheets of paper rolled up for their teacher on his or her return with the request that sometime at the end of the year, the teacher repeats this lesson to see how much, if any, class members have grown.

What's in a Name?

Grade Level: K–1

Approximate Time Required: 15 minutes

Purpose: To discuss the significance of a name in getting identity.

Materials: roll book

Individual Development & Identity

Directions: Tell students how you've been trying to learn all their names, and they've been learning your name, too. Names are important to people. Are there two people in this class that have the same first name? (If so, take time to notice this and how we distinguish between the two students.) Sometimes people are named after someone in their family or a special friend, or a person who is greatly admired. Do any of you know why you were given your special first name?

Allow time for volunteers to discuss this. One child may say she was named after an aunt or grandmother. Another may say he was named after his father's best friend in college.

Then repeat this with middle names. Discuss nicknames. Is someone whose name is Susan called "Sue" or "Suzie"? Is someone whose name is Bill called "Scooter" or "Junior"?

Finally move on to last names. In some families there may be more than one surname because of combined families. A mother may choose to keep her maiden name or use her maiden and married name as a hyphenated name. Discuss and accept as natural and normal all the variations on family names that come up.

Then talk about other names we give family members: Mom, Dad, Sis, Grandpa, Uncle Jim, etc. Talk about names we use for adults not in our family such as Mr. Garcia, Mrs. Kelley, Dr. Bob, etc.

Also discuss titles that we use with some people such as Reverend Thomas, Sister Margaret, Dr. Blackburn, Miss Boonin. Let the students give their ideas as to why we use these titles and when they think that they will be called Mr. _____ or Miss _____.

School Workers

Grade Level: K–1

Approximate Time Required: 15 minutes

Purpose: To discuss the needs of a school community and the jobs that people perform so that the life of the school runs smoothly and safely.

Individuals, Groups, Institutions

Materials: paper
crayons
envelopes

Directions: Bring the children together and discuss the life of the school community and the various jobs that people hold in the school that are needed to make things run smoothly. The following will probably come up for discussion: teachers, the principal, aides, the librarian, the cook and cook helpers, the custodians, the school secretary, school nurse, traffic guard, parent volunteers, etc. Discuss the responsibilities of each briefly and ask, "What can we do to make things easier for the people who work here?" Elicit from students ideas such as:

- To help the custodians, we can be sure to put paper towels into the wastebasket in the bathrooms. We can be careful in the cafeteria not to spill food on the floor. At the end of the day we can do things to make our classroom easier to clean. (Depending on the school, this might mean putting chairs up on tables and picking up debris from the floor, etc.)

- To help the librarian, we can return books to the right place on time. If there are lounging pillows, we can put them back in place before we leave a reading nook. To help the school secretary, we can remember to arrive at school on time and bring what we need from home so that we don't have to use the school telephone to call a parent or care-giver for something we've forgotten.

Invite each student to make a thank-you card for a school helper. Circulate and write the school person's name on an envelope so that the child can put the card inside when it is finished. If the child can write "thank you," those words may appear on the card as well as a colorful drawing. If a child is unsure which of the many school personnel to thank, suggest the name of a staff member who might not otherwise receive a card. At the end of the day, deliver the cards in their envelopes to the school secretary for distribution.

Transportation Collage

Grade Level: K–1

Approximate Time Required: 15 minutes

Purpose: To provide experience in identifying modes of transportation and of working together on a single project.

Materials: old magazines
large piece of chart paper
glue
scissors
For each student:
a copy of Land, Sea, and Air reproducible on page 49

Directions: Ask students to close their eyes for a moment and to imagine different ways that they could be moving about if they were in town or in the country right now. Then ask them to imagine how they might have moved about one hundred years ago. Have students open their eyes and discuss the ways they moved. Some may have imagined being in a car or on a bus or in a submarine. Others may have imagined a train or plane. Some may have thought of riding a horse, a stagecoach, being in a covered wagon, riding in a sailboat, or in a canoe. Allow each child to tell what mode of transportation he or she was imagining.

Then point to the big piece of chart paper and the stack of magazines. Give each pair of children a magazine and ask them to search for some means of transportation pictured in the magazine. Direct them to cut out the picture and bring it to you when they find one. Glue these pictures onto the chart paper, creating a collage called "Transportation." Encourage students to suggest where their picture might fit best on the collage. If time permits, allow students to cut more than one picture.

When the collage is filled with all sorts of pictures of the way people move about on land, on water, and in the air, take time to discuss whether the pictures show a way we move about in our modern world, whether it is a way (like the stage coach) which was only used in the past, or whether, like riding on horseback, it is a mode of transportation used today and also used in the past.

If the collage seems incomplete, you might suggest that students could look for pictures in old magazines at home, and with permission, cut them out and bring them in to add to the class transportation collage.

Once the collage is finished, have students complete the reproducible on various forms of transportation on page 49. They should cut out the vehicle pictures on the dotted lines and paste the pictures onto the Land, Sea, and Air illustration in the appropriate places.

Land, Sea, and Air

Name _____

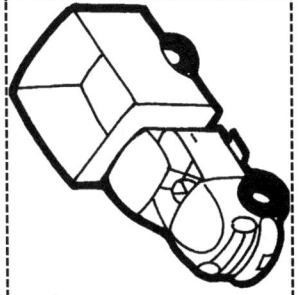

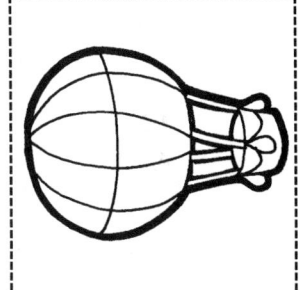

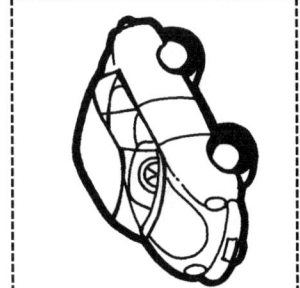

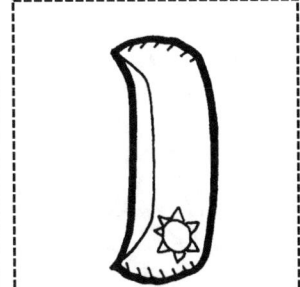

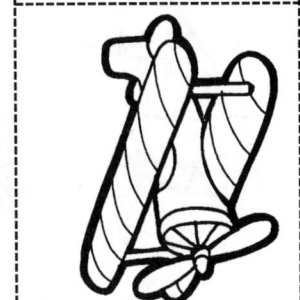

© Carson-Dellosa

CD-0048 *The Substitute's Own Survival Guide*

A Special Treat

Grade Level: K–1

Approximate Time Required: 20 minutes

Purpose: To describe foods of different cultural groups.

Culture

Materials: circles of paper

Directions: Gather the students into a comfortable area for a class discussion. Ask them to think about some special event that they celebrate in their family. It may be a birthday or a holiday celebration. Then ask them to think about foods that they eat on special occasions. Are there some special treats? Allow time for discussion.

Point out that people came to the United States of America from many parts of the world. Sometimes these people brought languages and special customs with them. Often they brought recipes for special foods from their "old country" to their "new country." Some of these foods are only made for special occasions. Sometimes people have recipes that were handed down from great-grandparents.

Some of these special dishes from other countries of the world have become favorites of many people in the United States. People who are not Asian may like to go out for Chinese, Korean, or Japanese food. People who are not French may enjoy French cooking. People who are not Greek or Italian may have a favorite Greek or Italian restaurant that they visit.

Ask students to discuss some of their favorite foods. Are any of these foods from an old family recipe? Are some associated with special ethnic holidays? Allow time for children to discuss.

Then hand a circle of drawing paper to each student. Ask each child to imagine that this circle is a dinner plate, and to draw on it a favorite food. If time permits, after each student has had a chance to draw food on the plate, bring the group together again and encourage volunteers to share and tell about their drawings.

Mixed-Up Animal

Grade Level: 2–3

Approximate Time Required: 20–30 minutes

Different Writing Process Elements

Purpose: To provide experience in using different writing process elements to create a page of a picture book for an audience of kindergarten students.

Materials: 12" x 18" pieces of manila construction paper
pencils
crayons

Directions: Explain to students that they are going to write a picture book which will be bound together and presented to a kindergarten class in the school. Each student will create one page for the book by drawing a picture of a mixed-up animal and writing about it.

Provide a model on the chalkboard to assist the children. As you say, "My animal is a hippo-giraffe," draw a rough sketch on the board. It might have a broad body of a hippo, with sturdy short legs, and the long neck of a giraffe, with knobs on top of its head. Beneath the picture write the following:

This mixed-up animal is a hippo-giraffe.
It eats the leaves of tall, green jungle trees.
When it is frightened or angry, it makes a whistling noise and stamps its feet.

Take time to brainstorm and write other ideas for combination animals on the chalkboard, such as zebra-ostrich, a rhino-gator, or a camel-ephant.

Instruct students to create their own "mixed-up animals," from two or three real animals, draw its picture, and write three or four sentences about the animal.

Collect the pages and bind them into a book. Using a marker, title the book CRAZY MIXED-UP ANIMALS. Ask a pair of student volunteers to design the cover for the book. Allow time for students in the class to look through this picture book before giving it to a kindergarten class in the school.

Baseball Spelling

Grade Level: 2–3

Approximate Time Required: 20 minutes

Purpose: To provide experience in correctly spelling and defining words in the context of a game.

Materials: a list of spelling words (one is provided on page 53)
a dictionary
a chalkboard
four chairs set up to designate home plate, first base, second base, third base

Directions: Designate one person as scorekeeper to keep score on the chalkboard. Line the rest of the class up divided into two teams. Play the part of the pitcher. Choose a word from the weekly spelling list or other source and "pitch" it by pronouncing it to the first person in line on one of the two teams. That first person tries to spell the word. If the person spells it correctly, that person moves to first base. Pitch another word to the next person on the team. If the second person spells the word correctly, he or she moves to first base, and the person on first advances to second base.

If a team member spells the word incorrectly, it counts as an out for the team, the players on base do not advance, and the person who missed the word goes to the end of the team line. Each time a person reaches home plate, one run is scored for the team. When a team has three outs, that half of the inning is over, and a word is pitched to the first person on the other team.

At any time, a player may announce that he or she is going to "hit a home run." This must be announced before the spelling word is pronounced. To hit a home run, the student must first spell the word correctly and then define it your satisfaction. If a person who declares that he or she is trying for a home run either spells the word correctly or fails to give an adequate definition, it is counted as an out for the team. You may wish to compare a dictionary definition with the definition provided by the student. The student definition certainly does not need to be exact but must clearly demonstrate knowledge of what the spelling word means.

At the end of play, the winning team is the team with the most runs.

List of Spelling Words for Grades 2–3

about	farm	kite	pulling	those
again	fast	knew	purple	thought
angry	father	know	quilt	three
animal	favorite	lamp	quit	tip
apart	feel	leave	quite	tonight
apple	felt	light	quitting	town
are	fight	line	rain	tree
arm	finish	lion	reach	trim
bean	first	log	really	tug
beautiful	food	look	red	twig
because	foot	lucky	ride	two
before	found	lunch	right	vase
below	friend	made	room	very
best	frown	mail	round	wanted
black	gem	make	row	was
blue	glass	map	school	we
book	gold	meat	shake	well
boot	good	mess	sister	went
bread	grass	milk	slow	were
bright	green	moon	small	what
broom	group	more	smart	wheel
brother	hard	mother	smile	when
brown	have	mouse	sometimes	where
bug	himself	myself	soon	who
can't	hook	name	spark	why
care	hoping	need	sports	will
cartoon	horse	nest	star	with
caught	house	new	start	won
charcoal	how	night	stop	won't
children	hurt	noon	story	wore
city	I'm	nothing	straight	work
clock	important	oak	sun	would
cookie	indeed	often	tall	write
could	its	orange	tell	writing
count	it's	order	thank	year
dark	jar	other	that	yearly
didn't	join	our	their	yell
down	joke	outside	them	yellow
draw	joy	path	then	yes
dress	jump	people	there	yet
drink	junk	person	these	you
eating	key	phone	they	you'll
empty	kick	planet	they're	young
every	kiss	play	thing	your
eyes	kitchen	pretty	think	zoo

I Remember

Grade Level: 2–3

Approximate Time Required: 20–30 minutes

Structure and Conventions

Purpose: To provide experience in writing a type of poem made popular by the poet Jack Collom and invented by Joe Brainard.

Materials: lined writing paper
pencils

Directions: Explain to students that they are going to write a different type of poem today. This poem, called an "I Remember" poem, does not rhyme and can have any number of lines of any length. Each line in the poem, however, begins with the words "I remember." Urge students to use details to bring life to their memories.

Brainstorm with students some of their vivid childhood memories and write these down in a few words on the chalkboard. Among those suggested might be: going to the hospital, winning a soccer game, getting a new bike, receiving a pet, having a special birthday party, sleeping away from home the first time, meeting a new baby brother or sister, learning to swim, or jumping off a diving board for the first time.

Encourage each student to write an "I remember . . ." poem. When they are completed, take the time to allow volunteers to share their poems with the class.

An example follows:

> I remember moving to a new town.
> I remember that the woman working at the post office
> already knew my name.
> I remember the people in the store
> looked curiously at me and then looked away.
> I remember not knowing anyone when I walked into church.
> I remember one old lady in a big hat who smiled at me.
> I remember wondering if I'd ever make new friends.
> I remember wishing I were back home again.

Acrostics

Grade Level: 2–3

Approximate Time Required: 20 minutes

Different Writing Process Elements

Purpose: To provide practice in using expressive language in communicating ideas through using an acrostic.

Materials: lined writing paper
pencil

For each student:
a copy of Various Forms of Poetry on page 56

Directions: Explain to students that they are going to write a different type of poem. The poem need not rhyme. The first letter of each line in the poem when read from top to bottom spells out the subject of the poem. Put this example on the chalkboard:

F lames leap high in the branches of trees.
O ld pine needles on the ground burst into flame.
R ocks become blazing hot,
E ager reporters wonder how this fire began.
S moke makes it hard to breathe.
T rees turn black.
F irefighters work to save a home,
I ntense heat forces them back.
R ain would be very welcome right now!
E very bird and animal flees the woods.

Encourage students to write their own acrostics. They may choose a one- or a two-word subject for their acrostic poem. If there is time, students may wish to illustrate their poem.

If time permits, encourage volunteers to share their poems with the class. Post the poems on a bulletin board display or in a class booklet.

Have students study the poetry examples on the reproducible and try their hand at creating some poems of their own.

Various Forms of Poetry

Alliterative Poetry

Alliteration is a device used to make poetry sound interesting. Everyone has heard the saying "Sally sells seashells at the seashore." Use alliteration (same beginning sound) to create your own alliterative poem.

Sunshine

The sun shone softly over Samantha's
shoulder, shimmering on the sea.
She sighed as she sat on the sweltering sand.

Cinquain

A cinquain is a five-line poem that describes something. The first line is a noun—the thing you want to describe. The second line is two words (adjectives) describing the first line. The third line contains three action words describing the first line. The fourth line is a sentence about the noun in line one. The last or fifth line is a single word that summarizes the noun mentioned in line one.

Jell-O
Jell-O
jiggly, wiggly
jelling, setting, flavoring
Jell-O is so delicious.
Yummy

Limerick

A limerick is a highly structured, generally humorous, poem in which lines one, two, and five rhyme and lines three and four rhyme.

There once was a farmer named Fred
who spent every day in bed.
When his hogs had grown fat,
in the barnyard they sat.
And Fred, he went broke, so they said.

Alliterative Poetry

_____

_____

_____

_____

Cinquain

_____

_____

_____

_____

_____

Limerick

_____

_____

_____

_____

_____

_____

Sneaky Shoe Adventure

Grade Level: 2–3

Approximate Time Required: 20 minutes

Purpose: To provide experience in writing an adventure story.

Materials: lined writing paper
pencils
crayons

Directions: Discuss with your students how they do many different things in a day. However, they probably haven't looked at a day's happenings from the point of view of an object like their own shoes. Explain that for this activity, instead of thinking of shoes as inanimate objects, students should pretend that shoes have thoughts and feelings and try to imagine what a day's adventures would be like when seen through the "eyes" a shoe.

For example, if on the way to school you stepped in a puddle of water or walked through mud or the remains of snow, what might that feel like to a shoe? If at recess you played kick ball and kicked a ball way out into the field, what might that feel like to a shoe? Suppose you had a turn on the swing and sailed high. How would the swishing air passing by feel to the shoe? What if at lunch time in the cafeteria you spilled milk on your shoe? How would that feel?

Once the students have the idea of writing about a typical day's adventures from the point of view of the shoe, ask each child to write a story. Some students might want to illustrate one scene of their story.

When everyone has had a chance to write an adventure story, provide time for volunteers to read their Sneaky Shoe Adventure to the class.

© Carson-Dellosa

CD-0048 *The Substitute's Own Survival Guide*

Add-On Story

Grade Level: 2–3

Approximate Time Required: 20 minutes

Purpose: To provide experience in careful listening and in creating an episodic story.

Materials: tape recorder
cassette tape
a large button
long piece of yarn or string

Directions: Sit with your class in a circle in a comfortable area of the room. Thread a button onto a long piece of string. Each student holds onto the piece of string. You should hold the string and the large button that is threaded onto the string.

Explain that the whole class will help to compose a story. Each person will add at least one sentence but may add several sentences to the story. Turn on the tape recorder so that there will be a record of the completed story. Begin the story and give the names of the characters and the setting to get the story under way.

For example, you might say, "It was Halloween night and three good friends named Bill, Bob, and Betty went out to trick-or-treat in a neighborhood that none of them had ever visited before. Bill was dressed as a ghost; Bob was dressed as Spider-Man; and Betty was dressed as a witch. They each carried a pillowcase to carry their treats, and they had already received lots of candy. They came to a house with a jack-o'-lantern shining in the window. Except for the jack-o'-lantern, the rest of the house was dark. Bill knocked on the door, and . . ."

At this point in the story, pass the button to the student sitting to the right, and that student continues the story, adding more and more elements. After a sentence or two, that student passes the button to the right, and another student takes up the story. This continues with everyone getting a turn. If the story ends before everyone has had a chance to participate, take the button and begin a new story. This time at an exciting point, pass the button to the left so that students who have not had a turn will get one.

Humorous Story

Grade Level: 2–3

Approximate Time Required: 20–30 minutes

Purpose: To provide experience in writing humor.

Materials: **For each student:**
    lined writing paper reproducible on page 61
    pencils
    crayons

Different Writing Process Elements

Directions: Explain to the class that people write for many different purposes. Sometimes they want to give information. Sometimes they want to explain how to do something. This activity involves trying to write a story that is humorous, one that will make people smile.

You may wish to share some parts of books checked out from the library as examples of humor. The Amelia Bedelia stories would work for this purpose. Read a portion of a humorous story aloud and then discuss some of the elements of humor.

Make short notes on the chalkboard as students share their ideas. They may suggest some of the following: humor can come from the unexpected, from a character getting mixed up or confused, from funny names or situations, or from exaggeration.

Then with the class, generate some elements for a possible humorous story. Your list might include the following:

Who? Pickle Face, Kooshy Wooshy, Knocka-Walka, Flat Pancake

Where? on a star, on the planet Pop-Pop-Ta-Ta, deep in the jungle, in a store

When? at midnight, at 12 noon, on Halloween, on your birthday

What? a musical instrument, a strange hat, an unusual animal, a new invention

When you have sufficient choices to work with, ask students to pick a who, where, when, and what from the chalkboard list and use these to write and illustrate a humorous short story on the reproducible paper provided on page 61. When complete, if time permits, invite volunteers to read their humorous stories aloud to the class.

Pocket Change

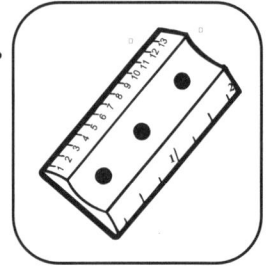

Grade Level: 2–3

Approximate Time Required: 10–20 minutes

Problem Solving

Purpose: To provide experience in problem solving using coins.

Materials: For each student:
paper
pencil
a copy of reproducible coins on page 63

Directions: Write the following on the chalkboard:
How many pennies, nickels, dimes, and quarters do you have in your pocket?

1. 3 coins add up to $.36
2. 7 coins add up to $ .27
3. 11 coins add up to $1.01
4. 4 coins add up to $ .25
5. 4 coins add up to $.70
6. 20 coins add up to $1.00
7. 6 coins add up to $ .30
8. 8 coins add up to $2.00
9. 10 coins add up to $ .50
10. 5 coins add up to $ .56

Students may cut out and use the coins from the reproducible to help them formulate their answers. After students have had a chance individually to write the answers to the questions on their papers, take time to go over the problems as a group, calling on volunteers to solve each question.

Favorite Colors

Grade Level: 2–3

Approximate Time Required: 20 minutes

Purpose: To provide experience in collecting and graphing data.

Materials: slips of paper

Data Analysis and Probability

Directions: Ahead of time, draw an incomplete bar graph on the chalkboard. Along the vertical axis are the numerals 0 to 15. Along the horizontal axis are colors such as red, green, yellow, blue, pink, orange, and purple. Tell students that they are going to gather data and then show the results of their survey in the form of a bar graph. Hand out a slip of paper to each student.

Point out that most people have favorite colors. They may often choose these colors for the clothes that they wear or for items to decorate their rooms. They may choose these colors as bright accents to wear with black and white clothing. Ask students to list their favorite colors and write these color names on the chalkboard. Then ask each student to pick a favorite from the colors listed and write this on the slip of paper handed out.

Choose two volunteers to collect the slips of paper and to put tally marks on the chalkboard after each color name.

List along the horizontal axis of the bar graph each of the colors that receives at least one vote from the class as a favorite color. Then ask for volunteers to come up and chalk in the results. For example, if six class members choose "yellow" as a favorite color, the student will go up the vertical axis to six and then color in a bar above the color yellow to the line indicating six. When completed, the bar graph will show at a glance the favorite class colors.

Follow up with a discussion of the data. Did one color emerge as a big favorite with the class? Did two colors tie as favorites?

Students may use the Favorite Color Survey reproducible on page 65 to survey friends outside their class and create their own bar graphs of results.

Favorite Color Survey

Ask your friends their favorite color and make a tally mark on the line for that color.

Red   _____

Green   _____

Yellow   _____

Blue   _____

Pink   _____

Orange   _____

Purple   _____

Make a bar graph of your results.

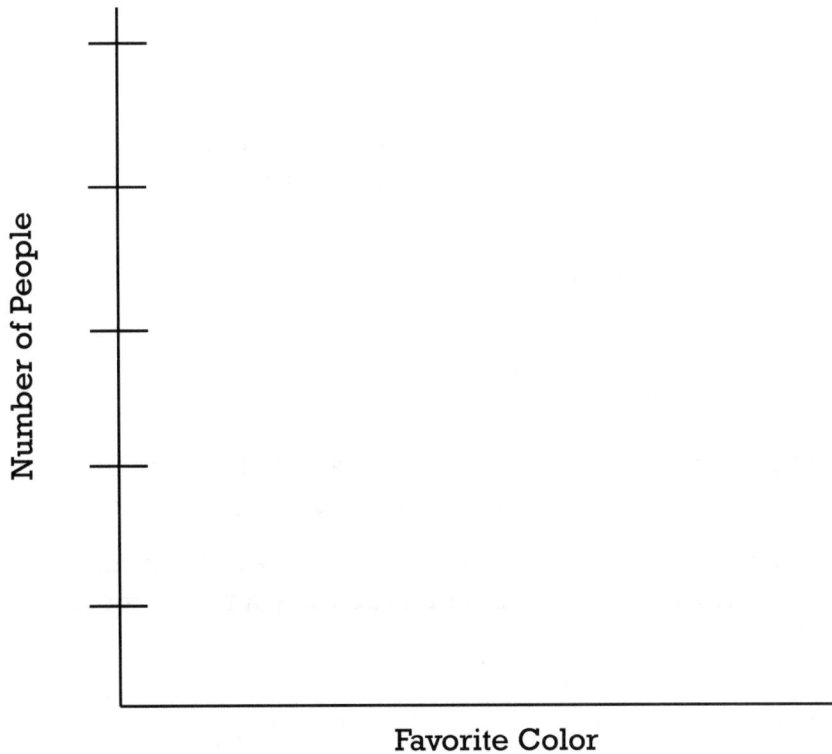

Number of People

Favorite Color

Classroom Measurement

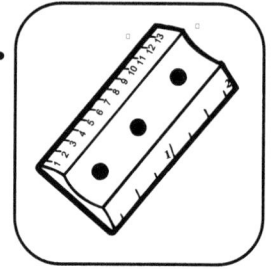

Grade Level: 2–3

Approximate Time Required: 10–20 minutes

Purpose: To provide experience in measuring.

Materials: yardsticks
tape measures
rulers
papers and pencils

Directions: Organize the students in small teams of two to four members. Each team will need to designate a recorder who will have paper and pencil. Each team will need a set of measuring tools.

Tell students that they are to measure various objects in the room and record those measurements to the nearest inch. Write the names of the following objects on the chalkboard:

> Carpet
> Door
> Top of teacher's desk
> Top of a table in the room
> Bulletin board

Ask students to decide as a team which measuring tools to use and how to carry out the measurement. Their recorder will record their measurements for each of the six items named on the chalkboard.

After the teams have completed their measurements, involve the students in a class discussion:

1. Did all teams get the same measurements?
   How might we explain any differences?

2. Did all teams use the same measuring tools to measure the same objects?
   Did the use of different tools yield different answers?

3. If you did not have rulers, yardsticks, or tape measures available, how might you estimate the length and width of the carpeted area of your classroom?

Mental Math

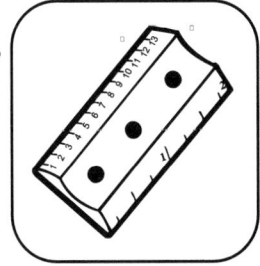

Grade Level: 2–3

Approximate Time Required: 15 minutes

Number and Operation

Purpose: To encourage appropriate use of mental math.

Materials: question list (below)
   paper and pencils

Directions: Explain that often students write down and solve problems, but sometimes they do mental math and solve problems in their head.

Tell them to write the numerals from one to four on their paper. Then read the four questions and have them answer each with "yes" or "no." They are not to write down the numbers and solve the problem. They should use mental math.

Wait while students put the numbers on their papers and then read the following:

1. If a cookie recipe calls for one-third cup of sugar and you plan to double the recipe to makes lots of cookies, do you need more than one cup of sugar?

2. You are buying a birthday present for a friend. You have $10 to spend. You are going to buy a beach towel and the price is $8.95. You look at cards. The cheapest birthday card is $1.95. Do you have enough money to buy both the present and the card?

3. The package of party napkins said that there were fifteen napkins in the package. One dozen people are coming to the party. Is one package of napkins enough?

4. There is going to be a class party. There are twenty-eight people in the class. Tom will bring sugar cookies; Mary will bring chocolate chips; and Bill will bring peanut butter cookies. If each brings two dozen cookies to the party, will there be enough cookies for every student to have three cookies?

Collect the papers. Then read the problems again, one by one, and call for volunteers to come to the chalkboard and show how they decided whether to answer the problem "yes" or "no."

Mystery Number

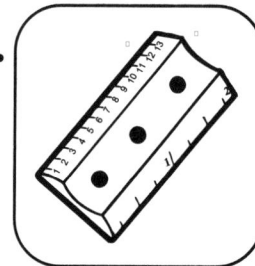

Grade Level: 2–3

Approximate Time Required: 10–20 minutes

Purpose: To provide experience in reasoning and problem solving.

Materials: paper and pencil

Directions: Read the clues given for problems one through four at the bottom of the page and allow students time to solve each problem. Students should write down their answers. After all four problems have been solved, call on a student to give the answer and explain how he or she went about solving the problem. If time permits, allow each student to write an original mystery problem. Students may volunteer to read their problems aloud while class members try to solve them.

1. I am a two-digit even number.
   I am smaller than sixty.
   I am bigger than twenty.
   One of my digits is even and one of my digits is odd.
   The sum of my digits is thirteen.
   I am _____. (fifty-eight)

2. I am a two-digit odd number.
   I am smaller than fifty.
   I am bigger than thirty.
   Both of my digits are odd.
   The sum of my digits is eight.
   I am _____. (thirty-five)

3. I am a two-digit number.
   One of my digits is four.
   You name me when you count to one hundred by tens.
   I am _____. (forty)

4. When you count to one hundred by fives, you say my name.
   I have two digits.
   My two digits are the same.
   I am _____. (fifty-five)

Patterns

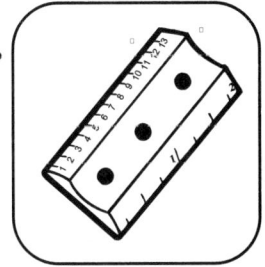

Grade Level: 2–3

Approximate Time Required: 20 minutes

Purpose: To provide experience in identifying recurring patterns.

Materials: a copy of the patterns chart below

Directions: Tell the class to look carefully up, down, and across the chart, looking for patterns. Some numerals are missing, but students should be able to figure out which ones they are. Then students should follow the directions below.

1		3		5		7	8		10
11	12			15			18		20
21		23				27			30
31			34				38		40
41	42			45				49	50
51		53			56				60
61			64			67		69	70
71	72			75			78		80
81		83			86				90
91			94			97		99	100

1. Count by threes and color each box yellow that you name as you count.

2. Count by fives and color each box green that you name as you count.

3. Which boxes look blue because you colored them both yellow and green?

The Summer Picnic

Grade Level: 2–3

Approximate Time Required: 20 minutes

Purpose: To provide experience in reasoning and problem solving

Materials: For each student:
    pieces of paper

Reasoning and Proof

Directions: Tell students that they are to pretend to plan for a summer family picnic in the park. Students are to listen to the problems below as you read them and then answer the questions either "yes" or "no." If they wish, they may draw pictures to help arrive at their answer.

1. There are nine people in the family: mother, father, three children, Aunt Mary, Uncle Jim, Grandma and Grandpa. Father is going to grill hamburgers. He can make four burgers from each pound of ground meat. If he buys two pounds of ground hamburger meat, will he have enough meat to make nine quarter pound hamburgers? (No)

2. Aunt Mary is bringing fruit. She will buy apples, bananas, and oranges. She wants to bring enough fruit so that everyone can have two pieces of fruit during the day. If she bought six apples, six bananas, and six oranges, will she have enough fruit? (Yes)

3. Grandma baked cookies. Her recipe makes two dozen cookies. She wants everyone to be able to have three cookies. Will one batch of cookies be enough? (No)

4. Grandpa is spreading out blankets so that people can sit on the ground. Four people will fit on each blanket. If he spreads out two blankets, will that be enough? (No)

5. Uncle Jim is bringing ice cold soda pop to drink. He will bring four flavors. He wants everyone to be able to have two soda pops during the afternoon. If he brings 6 cans of pop of each of the 4 flavors, will he have enough soda pop? (Yes)

Favorite Sports

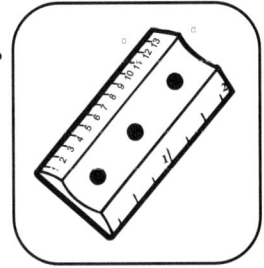

Grade Level: 2–3

Approximate Time Required: 20 minutes

Purpose: To provide experience in collecting and graphing data and in working with fractions.

Materials: slips of paper
chalkboard
chalk

Directions: Hand out slips of paper to each student. Draw a circle on the chalkboard. Tell students that they are going to gather data and then show the results of their sports survey in the form of a circle graph.

Point out that many people play sports professionally, some play for fun, and others like to watch sports in person or via television. Some people like lots of sports while others like very few. Elicit from the class names of sports that they like to play or watch. The following may be among those that are listed on the chalkboard: baseball, basketball, bowling, field hockey, football, golf, ice hockey, soccer, and tennis.

Ask each student to choose a favorite sport from the list and write it on the slip of paper. Call on two students to collect and count the votes, indicating by tally marks the number of fans for each sport.

Help students to change the tally marks into numbers and then simple fractions. If there are twenty-five students in the class and ten list football as their favorite sport, 10/25 or 2/5 of the class chose football as the favorite sport. Help students to figure out the fractions. (These can be exact or "approximate." If, for example, nine out of twenty-five students choose football, you can call this 9/25, divide the circle graph into twenty-five pieces and color nine of the pieces for football fans. Or you could consider 9/25 as almost 10/25 or almost 2/5 of the circle graph, and mark it accordingly.)

Then use the circle on the chalkboard as a circle graph. Give it a name: Favorite Sports to Watch or Play. Divide the circle into appropriate sections to show what fraction of the class chose each sport. (Most will choose baseball, football, basketball, and soccer. If only a very few choose golf or tennis you might lump some sports together as "other." Otherwise, you will have some "singletons" to show as 1/25 of the circle.) Help students see how to construct a circle graph.

The Weight of Air

Grade Level: 2–3

Approximate Time Required: 10–20 minutes

Purpose: To encourage students to inquire and to make observations of a simple science experiment that demonstrates that air has weight.

Materials:
a yardstick or meter stick
a ruler
a stack of books
a short piece of string
two balloons of identical size

Directions: First engage the class in discussion. Is there air in the classroom? How do we know there is air if we can't see, smell, or taste it? What have students observed which confirms their belief that air is all around? Do they think that air has weight?

Tell them that you will conduct a simple experiment and that they can observe and then determine the answer to that question.

On a desk or table, have students set two stacks of books (such as dictionaries) with three in each stack so that the stacks are the same height and are about two feet apart. Between the stacks of books, place a yardstick. Then across the yardstick, at right angles, place a ruler. This ruler should be placed so that its mid-point rests in the middle of the yardstick so that the ruler balances.

Let students take turns in showing that the ruler will continue to be in balance if objects of the same weight are placed at each end of the ruler, but that it will tip if weight is added to one side and not the other. Students might try various small objects in the classroom to demonstrate this.

Then ask, "If I tape a balloon (uninflated) at each end of the ruler, will it still be balanced?"

Tape an uninflated balloon to each end of the ruler with a small piece of masking tape and demonstrate that the ruler still balances because the same weight has been added to each end of the ruler.

Next, remove one of the balloons. Blow it up. Tie it with a short piece of string so that air can't escape and tape it back to the end of the ruler. Ask the students, "When I put the ruler back on the yardstick, will it still balance or not?" To a student who thinks that the ruler will no longer balance, ask "Why won't it balance any more?"

Place the ruler with one balloon blown up and one not blown up back on the yardstick. It will no longer balance. This demonstration will show that air has weight.

Making a New Constellation

Grade Level: 2–3

Approximate Time Required: 20–30 minutes

Earth and Space Science

Purpose: To provide experience in seeing that constellations, or groups of stars in the sky, often get their name from their shape.

Materials: a book of common constellations
a table covered with newspaper for protection
a paint shirt
a paintbrush
black tempera paint
large sheets of white art paper

Directions: Show one or two constellations from the book to the class and take the time to listen to other students who may know and want to talk about additional constellations of stars. Point out that people often make up stories about the constellations that they see in the sky and that people in different parts of the world make up different stories, depending on what they see as the star patterns.

Suggest that today, each student will have a turn in making a star pattern. Demonstrate how when it is a student's turn, he or she puts on a paint shirt, dips the paintbrush into the paint, holds the brush right above the white sheet of paper, and taps very gently, which will cause the black paint to splatter into specks on the paper. The student then carries the speckled paper to his or her desk to dry. Another child takes a turn at dipping the paintbrush and gently spattering a piece of paper and carries it to his or her desk to dry. Stress that a gentle tap is all that is necessary or too much paint will spatter onto the paper.

Read the class a story about one of the constellations while students take turns in spattering the paint.

When all students have had a turn spattering paint, have them go to their seats, look at their paper, and see if they can find a pattern of an object in their spatter painting. Once they have one, they should use a pencil to connect the spatter dots to form a constellation. They should name the constellation and write this on their paper. They might make up a short legend about their constellation.

As time permits, encourage volunteers to show their constellations to the rest of the students and to tell their legends.

Keeping in the Heat

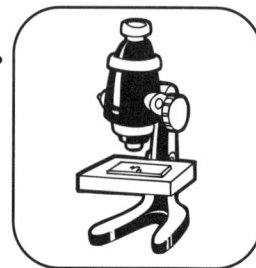

Grade Level: 2–3

Approximate Time Required: 30 minutes

Physical Science

Purpose: To show that covering a space slows the loss of heat.

Materials: two thermometers
two empty mayonnaise or other wide-mouth jars
a piece of plastic wrap
a rubber band
chalk
chalkboard

Directions: Explain to students that they are going to learn the effect that a covering has on heat and heat retention.

Have student volunteers label one jar as jar #1 by taping a #1 on the side of the jar. Tape #2 on the side of the other jar. Put a thermometer in each jar and place them side by side in a sunny window. Note the thermometer readings. List jar #1 and jar #2 on the chalkboard. Note the time and the temperature shown on the thermometers. Put a piece of clear plastic wrap over the opening of jar #2 and hold it in place tightly with a rubber band.

Wait five minutes and have two students record time and temperature beneath each jar listing on the chalkboard. Do this again after fifteen minutes.

Then take both jars out of the sunny window and put them in a dark closet side by side. Note the time and temperature after five, ten, and fifteen minutes. Gather students where they can read the results on the chalkboard and discuss what happened. They will see that the jar covered in plastic warmed up faster than the uncovered jar did. They will also note that the jar covered in plastic was slower to cool down when it was placed in the dark closet than the uncovered jar.

During the discussion, point out that when a casserole is taken out of the oven, it stays warm longer if the lid is kept on. Lids on "to go" orders of coffee or fast food help to keep contents hot for a longer period than they would be uncovered. Also, the gases in Earth's atmosphere act something like the plastic wrap on the jar. These gases let sunlight in and allow the earth to keep some of the heat. If our planet did not have an atmosphere, it would usually be cold and lose heat quickly.

Sunken Marbles

Grade Level: 2–3

Approximate Time Required: 15 minutes

Physical Science

Purpose: To provide experience in learning about density and volume and in making predictions.

Materials: a graduated two-cup measuring cup
24 marbles of the same size
a pitcher with tap water in it
a chalkboard
chalk
paper and pencil

Directions: Gather students in a position where they can see what is happening during this experiment. Pour water from the pitcher into the measuring cup to the level of eight ounces or one cup of water. Hold it up so that students can see that the water level reaches exactly one cup. On the chalkboard write "eight oz. of water."

Ask the class what will happen to the level of the water if you drop six marbles into the measuring cup. (Most students will suggest that the water level will rise because the marbles will take up space in the water.) Add six marbles to the cup of water. Note that the water level rises and write on the chalkboard the new level of the water in the measuring cup.

Then ask what will happen if you drop six more marbles into the measuring cup? (Students will almost all guess that the water will rise.) Drop six more marbles into the cup, note the level of the water in the measuring cup now, and write this new measurement on the chalkboard.

Tell the class that you are going to ask each person to make a prediction. First, look at the chalkboard and see the level of water with six marbles and with twelve marbles. Then make a guess as to what the level of water in the measuring cup will be after you add twelve more marbles to the cup of water. Wait while each student writes down his or her prediction. Collect the predictions. Ask for a pair of student volunteers to tally the predictions. One will read the prediction and the other will write on the chalkboard, keeping a tally of how many people made each prediction.

Drop another twelve marbles into the measuring cup of water. Note the level of the water and write this on the chalkboard. Did the majority of students make the correct prediction? Ask students to verbalize how they made their predictions.

Trick Your Sense of Taste

Grade Level: 2–3

Approximate Time Required: 20 minutes

Physical Science

Purpose: To show that the ability to taste is affected by the sense of smell.

Materials: pieces of raw potato, apple, and onion
paper cups
a blindfold
chalkboard

Directions: Set the stage by discussing the sense of smell. Ask students to recall some of their favorite smells. They may suggest the smell of a pie or cookies in the oven, a particular shampoo, perfume, or a bouquet of flowers.

Suggest that smell also helps us to enjoy the foods that we eat. Call for a volunteer. Put a blindfold on the volunteer and ask him/her to sit in a chair in front of the other class members. Tell the student that you will put a small piece of food on his or her tongue. The child is to try to guess what the food is by the taste without chewing on it. Before putting any food on the student's tongue, ask the child to pinch his/her nose closed so that the sense of smell will not be used.

Place a small piece of potato on the student's tongue (while the student is blindfolded and pinching his/her nose closed). Have him or her remove the piece of potato and discard it in a paper cup. Then put a piece of apple on the student's tongue and repeat the procedure. Finally put a piece of onion on the tongue and repeat the procedure. Between each taste test, the student tries to guess what food is placed on the tongue. Write the guesses on the chalkboard.

Repeat with two other volunteers. Change the order in which the potato, apple, and onion are placed on the tongue. Record these guesses on the chalkboard.

Repeat the test with three more volunteers. Continue to use the blindfold, but this time do not have these volunteers pinch their noses closed. Record their guesses on the chalkboard.

Do students do better, the same, or worse at guessing the foods when they are able to use their sense of smell?

Make a Rainbow

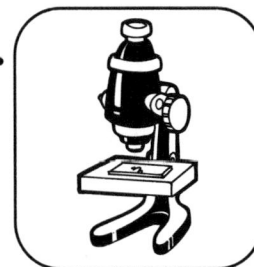

Grade Level: 2–3

Approximate Time Required: 10–20 minutes

Physical Science

Purpose: To show that water drops can bend white light and break it into different colors.

Materials:
- a window
- a shallow pan
- water
- a mirror
- a sheet of white paper

Directions: Choose a sunny day for this experiment. Fill a shallow pan with water and place it on a table in front of a sunny window. Place a small mirror in the water at the end of the pan facing the window.

Gather students in a semi-circle around the table, facing the window, where they will be able to see a white sheet of paper held by a student. The student holds a sheet of white paper with one edge resting on the table between the window and the pan of water. Slowly tilt the mirror back and forth to catch the light at different angles as it passes through the water and hits the mirror. The light will reflect from the mirror, pass through the water, and bend. When the mirror is angled just the right way, the light will bend enough to make a rainbow that will appear on the white paper.

This experiment can be followed up by a discussion of where students have seen rainbows:

> in the sky after a rain
> in the spray of water from a sprinkler
> in mist from waterfalls

Explain that sunlight contains all the colors of the rainbow, but they are blended together to make white light. Grass looks green to us, because only the green light is reflected to our eyes and the other colors are absorbed by the grass.

The children may wish to make a rainbow using markers or crayons: red, orange, yellow, green, blue, indigo violet.

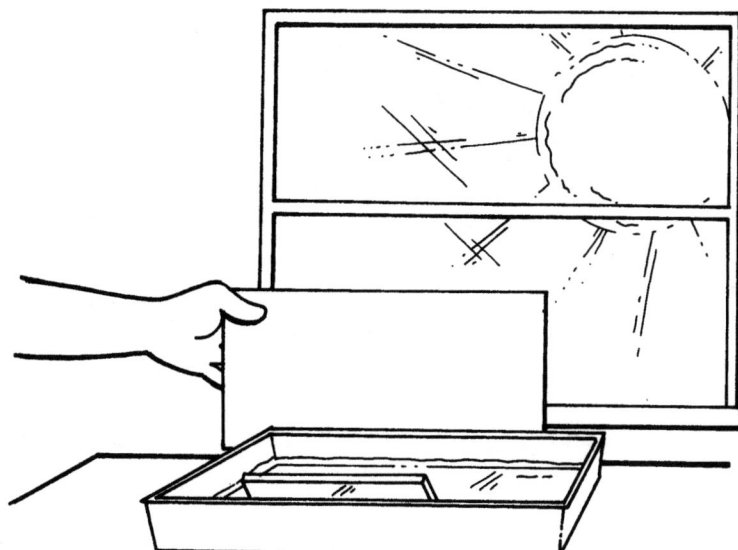

Floating and Sinking

Grade Level: 2–3

Approximate Time Required: 20 minutes

Purpose: To provide experience in observing which items float and which sink.

Physical Science

Materials: 4 baking pans of water
a spoon
salt
various small objects such as corks, paper clips, blocks, nuts, bolts, washers
a roll of foil
paper and pencil

Directions: Set up four work stations. Each will have a pan of water, a spoon, salt, and various small objects such as corks, paper clips, blocks, nuts, bolts, and washers. Each table will also need paper and pencil for recording observations.

Invite students to experiment with floating and sinking and to keep a record of what they observe. Suggest that before they place an object in the water, they first predict whether it will float or sink. They should experiment and record the results. The students, might, for example, write that the cork floats, and the washer sinks. After a few minutes, discuss what students observed.

Give each group a piece of foil about ten inches square. Suggest that they can mold the foil into a boat or raft and experiment to see if objects that sank will now float if put into the boat. After a few minutes, discuss what the students observed. Does the size and shape of the boat matter? Can a student make the foil sink?

Finally, suggest that the students add a tablespoonful of salt to their pan of water, stir with a spoon until the salt is dissolved and dispersed throughout the water, and repeat their experiments to see if objects sink or float differently in salt water. After a few minutes, discuss what students observed.

During the discussion, students will use their own words to explain that objects that are more dense than water will sink in water while objects that are less dense will float. Objects are more buoyant in salt water. Students will see that whether or not an object floats depends on how much space it occupies and from what material it is made.

Good for You!

Citizenship

Grade Level: 2–3

Approximate Time Required: 20–30 minutes

Purpose: To identify examples of good citizenship.

Materials: white construction paper
chalkboard and chalk
a certificate

   (If a blank model certificate is available, this would be helpful to hold up and show to students so they can see fancy borders and gold seals.)

Directions: Gather students together in a comfortable discussion area in the room. Tell students you have observed several examples of good citizenship throughout the day. (Cite some observed examples of one student in the room being polite, helpful, or considerate to another student, or of a task that was well done such as handing out books, erasing the chalkboard, etc.)

   Point out that although you saw many examples of good citizenship, there were probably many other examples that went unnoticed. These may have happened at school today or earlier in the week. Students may have observed examples of their classmates being responsible citizens in the library, during a music, art, or physical education period; at recess; while walking to or from school in the morning; or during the lunch period.

   Show students a sample of a certificate if you have one available. Point out that a certificate is usually a fancy document. Design the format you wish to use together.

Write the following on the chalkboard:

Certificate of Good Citizenship

Presented to _____ (student's name) _____ **on** _____ (date) _____

at _____ (name of school) _____ **for showing good citizenship by**

_____ (brief description of the act of good citizenship) _____

by _____ (name of student presenting certificate) _____

Allow time for each student to design and present a Certificate of Good Citizenship.

Community Helpers—Firefighters

Individuals,
Groups,
Institutions

Grade Level: 2–3

Approximate Time Required: 15–20 minutes

Purpose: To discuss the needs of a community and the jobs that people have that make the life of the community run smoothly and safely.

Materials: For each student:
reproducible fire safety poster paper on page 81
crayons

Directions: Bring students together and discuss some of the workers in a community that are needed to make things run smoothly. Students may mention firefighters, police officers, postal workers, etc. Take the time to discuss each briefly. Then begin a discussion about the work of firefighters and what can be done to keep safe from fires.

Discuss firefighters and the type of work they do. Review fire safety. Encourage students to come up with ideas such as: Do not play with matches. Don't cook or turn on the stove unless there is an adult to supervise. Always be careful around candles. If you see worn spots on the cord of a lamp or toaster where wires are showing, point this out to adults in the house. Be very careful with Fourth of July sparklers and other fireworks and only use these when adults are present. If you go camping, be sure to completely put out campfires. If people smoke in your house, be sure that they have ashtrays to use and do not put cigarettes in wastepaper baskets. With your family, plan what to do in the event of a fire. What route should you take to get out? Know your address and how to call 911.

Give students each a copy of the reproducible poster paper on page 81. Ask them to write one sentence relating to fire safety. The sentence might read, "Always be sure your campfire is completely out." Once the sentence is written, ask each student to draw and color a picture to go with it.

Once all the students have written their sentences and colored their pictures, gather all the pages and staple them into a fire safety book. One or two children might volunteer to make a cover for the book. For example, they might cut red and orange flames from construction paper and glue these onto a white cover page.

Name_____

Places on a Map

Grade Level: 2–3

Approximate Time Required: 10 minutes

Space and Place

Purpose: To provide experience in tracing a journey on a map.

Materials: Make a copy of the map on the next page for each student in the class.

Directions: Give each student a copy of the map on the following page and ask them to take out a red crayon and be prepared to trace a route on the map. Ask students to listen carefully while they mark the path that Erin follows to reach her home.

When school is out for the day, Erin goes home. But instead of taking the shortest path between school and home, Erin takes the long way home, dropping friends off at their houses along the way. Use a red crayon to mark Erin's path.

1. The school is on the northwest corner of First Avenue and Adams Street. Erin walks to the corner of 1st Avenue and Brown Street.

2. She then walks three blocks east. She does not cross Fourth Avenue but instead walks south for two blocks.

3. She walks west for one block.

4. Then she turns south and goes one block.

5. She turns east for one block.

6. Then she goes south for one block.

7. Finally, she walks three blocks west to her house. She lives on the west side of the street.

8. Now use a green crayon to show the shortest route that Erin might have followed to get quickly from the school to her house.

Places on a Map

Adams Street

Brown Street

Curtis Street

1st Avenue 2nd Avenue 3rd Avenue 4th Avenue

Davis Street

Evans Street

Fern Street

Once...But Now...

Grade Level: 2–3

Approximate Time Required: 30 minutes

Purpose: To provide experience in recording maturation.

Materials: For each student:
      a copy of the Once...But Now... reproducible on page 85
      scissors
      construction paper
      stapler

Individual Development & Identity

Directions: Discuss with students the changes they have experienced from birth to the present time. As students suggest ideas, record these on the chalkboard in the following form:

Once I had very little blonde hair.
Now, I have lots of light brown hair that I wear in a pony tail.

Once I had no teeth.
Now I have lots of teeth.

Once I could not talk.
Now I talk all the time.

Once I could not walk.
Now I can walk, run, and ride a bike, too.

After going through several examples such as the above, ask students to write their own, "Once . . . But Now . . ." booklet. Have them design a cover from a piece of 8" x 10" construction paper folded in half and include their first and last name on the cover. Then they should fill the booklet with the Once . . . But Now . . . pages from the reproducible on page 85 with similar content to those suggested above. Students should complete the sentences in their booklets at the bottom of each page and should draw their illustrations above the sentences. Then they may cut out the individual pages and staple them into their construction paper covers to form booklets.

If time permits, gather the class together and invite volunteers to read their "Once . . . But Now . . ." booklets to the class.

Once I had . . .
Now I have . . .

Once I had . . .
Now I have . . .

Once I had . . .
Now I have . . .

Once I had . . .
Now I have . . .

Community Helpers— Police Officers

Grade Level: 2–3

Approximate Time Required: 20 minutes

Purpose: To discuss the needs of a community and the jobs that people have that make the life of the community run smoothly and safely.

Materials: a police officer's cap (optional)   **For each student:** a copy of the reproducible on page 87

Directions: Bring the children together and discuss some of the people in the community that are needed to make things run smoothly. Students may mention firefighters, police officers, postal workers, etc. Take the time to discuss each briefly. Then discuss in detail what members of the police force do to help the community.

Read the following scenario to students:

Suppose that you have gone downtown to see a big parade. Imagine that you went with your mother or father but that so many people came that somehow you got separated from your parent and you became lost. You might first stand still and look around carefully trying to find your parents. But imagine that your parents are still nowhere to be seen and that a police officer in a uniform comes up to you and asks, "May I help you?"

What sorts of questions would the police officer ask, and what kind of information would you need to know to help the police officer safely get you back with your parents again?

Ask for volunteers to act out the roles of the police officer and the lost child. Let several students take turns trying out these roles. Discuss what sorts of questions are helpful and what kind of information is needed in this situation. Also point out how you identify a police officer and distinguish between a police officer and a complete stranger.

Have students complete the reproducible on page 87, explaining what they want to be when they grow up.

What do you want to be when you grow up?

_____

_____

Why?

_____

_____

_____

_____

_____

_____

_____

_____

_____

_____

Postal Service

Grade Level: 2–3

Approximate Time Required: 15–20 minutes

Individuals, Groups, Institutions

Purpose: To discuss the needs of a community and the various jobs that people have which help make the life of the community run smoothly and safely.

Materials: envelopes to address
small "treats" such as a crackers

Directions: Bring the students together and discuss some of the workers in a community that are needed to make any community run smoothly. Students may mention firefighters, police officers, postal workers, etc. Take the time to discuss each briefly. Then discuss what postal workers do to help the community.

Have students point out ways in which they or their family members use the postal service. They may discuss receiving packages from relatives on birthdays, sending a greeting card to a friend or relative, receiving bills at home for various services, receiving catalogues for various products, or sending a letter to a pen pal in another state or a foreign country.

Take the time to discuss how sending and receiving messages and packages has changed over the years. The following topics may arise in this discussion: e-mail, UPS, FAX machines, and the telephone. Point out that for a letter or package to arrive safely through the postal service, the address must be clear and complete. Elicit from the class the following format:

> Name of the student
> Name of the school
> Street number and address of the school
> City, two-letter state abbreviation, and ZIP code of the school

Ask each student to address an envelope in the correct format. Then have the students bring their envelopes to a table where they may take a graham cracker or other small treat from a box, put it in the envelope, seal it, and deposit it in a box.

Once all the stuffed and addressed envelopes are in the box, ask for volunteers to be mail carriers. Have these volunteers each take two or three envelopes from the box and deliver them to classmates. When all envelopes have been delivered, students may open their mail and enjoy the treats.

The Monthly Special

Grade Level: 4–5

Approximate Time Required: 20 minutes

Purpose: To practice writing for a specific purpose and for a special audience in a persuasive way.

Materials: scratch paper
pen or pencil
crayons
markers or colored pencils
a piece of oaktag
an apple

Directions: Ask the class members to imagine that they work in the advertising and promotions department of a famous chain of restaurants. Their job is to come up with a great idea that will be featured all over the country next month as "The Monthly Special" at each of the restaurants in the chain. They are to dream up, provide a catchy name, draw, and describe a special dish that will be a mouth-watering treat. This treat must contain apples in some form. Show students the apple.

Suggest that on scratch paper they make a sketch of this treat and jot down words that describe it and will inspire customers to order this. They should also try out several "catchy" names to help generate interest in the product.

After they have their ideas in mind, each student should draw this specialty dish using colored pencils, crayons, or markers and describe it in glowing terms so that customers all over the country will be unable to resist ordering it. This final advertisement should be made on the sheet of oaktag, folded in half, so that it could be placed on a counter or restaurant table as a "tent" advertisement that will stand up and draw attention to "The Monthly Special."

If time permits, have students each place their complete tent advertisement on their desk or table and let them move about the room and read the various descriptions of "The Monthly Special." If you wish, you could give each of the students a slip of paper as a ballot and ask them to vote for their favorite monthly special. (The prize could be awarding the apple that you held up at the beginning of the lesson for the prize.)

Evocative Pictures

Grade Level: 4–5

Approximate Time Required: 30 minutes

Purpose: To provide students practice in using language structure and appropriate conventions of spelling and punctuation to create dialogue in text.

Materials: pencil or pen and paper
six photos cut from magazines
These might include such things as:
an elderly person sitting on a porch
a cowboy riding a horse
a child sporting a Band-aid
someone inside looking out the window at the rain
an isolated cabin covered in snow

Directions: First, review on the chalkboard the accepted conventions for using dialogue in a story. (There is an indentation and new paragraph each time there is a change of speaker. The words spoken aloud are included in quotation marks, and punctuation goes within the quotation marks.)

As an example, write the following sentences on the chalkboard:

"I smell something good," Billy said.

"I do, too," said Mary.

They ran into the house and went to the kitchen where they found Grandma taking cookies out of the oven. "Hungry?" Grandma asked.

After reviewing the appropriate conventions for using dialogue in a story, ask the class members to choose one of the photographs displayed in the front of the room and use it as the starting point for a short story. The story might be realistic or fanciful. One requirement is that the story must contain some dialogue, and this dialogue must be correctly punctuated. When the lesson is complete, students might volunteer to read their stories to the class. The short stories may be placed on a bulletin board in a cluster around the magazine pictures which inspired the stories.

Haiku

Grade Level: 4–5

Approximate Time Required: 10–20 minutes

Purpose: To reflect upon and select words that work together to create a nature poem.

Materials: a haiku
a chalkboard
paper
pen or pencil

For each student:
a copy of the Haiku reproducible on page 92

Sample Haiku
Noisy bullfrog croaks
Making special spring music
That fills the soft night.

Directions: First write the haiku above on the chalkboard. Use it to review (or teach) students the syllable count needed for a haiku:

Haiku consists of 17 syllables in only 3 lines.

Line 1: 5 syllables
Line 2: 7 syllables
Line 3: 5 syllables

Have students write two haikus on the reproducible page 92. Have them star the one they like best. If time permits, encourage those students who wish to do so to read their favorite haiku aloud.

All the papers may be collected and the starred ones published as a class book of poetry. They could be illustrated and mounted on a classroom bulletin board. A tape recording could be made on which each student says his or her name and reads a favorite haiku.

Haiku

A New Just So Story

Grade Level: 4–5

Approximate Time Required: 30 minutes

Purpose: To provide experience in using different writing process elements to create a "just so" story in the spirit of Rudyard Kipling.

Materials: a collection of Rudyard Kipling's "Just So Stories," or a recording

Directions: Read to the class or play a recording of one of Rudyard Kipling's "Just So Stories." Read or tell one of these stories such as "How the Rhinoceros Got His Skin," "The Elephant Child," or "How the Whale Got His Throat." Take time to discuss the effective use of repetition and the word choices that Kipling makes which add to the quality of his stories. Notice how Kipling plays with language and blends in humor and surprise.

Ask students to brainstorm some of the animals that they like and to choose an outstanding feature of each animal. Write their suggestions on the chalkboard.

You might come up with a list something like this:

an owl's big eyes
a kangaroo's pocket
a snake's legless body
a parrot's brightly-colored feathers
a giraffe's long neck
a turtle's shell
a peacock's tail
a butterfly's colorful wings
a rhino's horn
a zebra's stripes

Invite each student to write an original "Just So Story" a la Rudyard Kipling. The student may wish to add an illustration to the story. The completed stories could be bound in a classroom book, or, if time permits, students could volunteer to read their stories to the class.

Puzzle It Out

Grade Level: 4–5

Approximate Time Required: 10–20 minutes

Purpose: To provide experience in solving a puzzle based on knowledge of language structure, frequency of vowels, double letters, singletons, etc.

Materials: reproducible of coded message on page 95
pencil

Directions: Hand out a copy of the reproducible coded message to each student. Students will try to crack the code and solve the puzzle.

Explain that the coded message is a quotation from a famous person. It is a substitution code where one letter of the alphabet is substituted for another letter of the alphabet. The code can be cracked by using a knowledge of words and structure. For example, each of the words must contain a vowel. Can you figure out where the vowels are? Certain letters are commonly doubled (such as ee). Singletons will have to be the letter "a" or "I." Students should write below the coded message the letters that spell out the message. (If you wish, give a few hints such as: A = S, C = N, and Z = H.)

AHPG	LGHLXG	AGG	EZDCFA	BA	EZGU
Some	people	see	things	as	they

BYG	BCN	BAS	I ZU	D	NYGBP
are	and	ask,	Why?	I	dream

NYGBPA	EZBE	CGMGY	I GYG	BCN	BAS
dreams	that	never	were	and	ask,

I ZU	CHE
Why?	not?

FGHYFG	JGYCBYN	AZBI
George	Bernard	Shaw

Crack That Code

AHPG   LGHLXG   AGG

____   _____   ___

EZDCFA   BA   EZGU   BYG

_____   __   ____   ___

BCN   BAS   IZU   D   NYGBP

___   ___ ,   ___ ?   _   _____

NYGBPA   EZBE   CGMGY   IGYG

_____   ____   _____   ____

BCN   BAS   IZU   CHE

___   ___ ,   ___   ___ ?

FGHYFG   JGYCBYN   AZBI

_____   _____   ____

Library Spelling Bee

Grade Level: 4–5

Approximate Time Required: 10–20 minutes

Purpose: To reinforce correct spelling of words often used in connection with the school library.

Materials: spelling words listed below (plus additional ones of your own choosing) chalkboard

Directions: Divide the class randomly into four groups. Name these teams blue, green, orange, and red. Ask for a volunteer to serve as scorekeeper. On the chalkboard write the names of the four teams: blue, green, orange, and red. Have each team line up in front of one of the classroom walls. Tell them that you are going to conduct a spelling bee. The words will be words commonly used in finding and checking out books and doing research in the library.

Say a word from the list below. Use the word in a sentence. Finally, you will repeat the word. Call on the first person on the blue team. That person spells the word. If he or she spells it correctly, say "correct." The scorekeeper then puts down one point for the blue team. Give a new word to the first person on the green team. If the student spells it correctly, tell him or her that it is correct, and the scorekeeper puts down one point for the green team. Continue around the room, giving words to the orange and red teams. Then continue in the same order. If a student misses a word, tell the student it is incorrect, and the scorekeeper does not add a point for the team. Give the same word to the next team.

At the end of the spelldown, the winning team might get a simple reward such as being first to line up for recess, lunch, or to go home at the end of the day. If there is a tie, a "sudden death" tie-breaker could be held. Give words to only members of the two teams that are tied. The first team to miss a word is the loser.

List of Library-Related Words for the Spelldown

biography	illustrator	editor
fiction	spine	copyright
author	publisher	reference
foreword	thesaurus	illustration
index	dictionary	shelf
contents	encyclopedia	bibliography
glossary	magazine	nonfiction
footnote	prologue	media

Seasonal Poetry

Grade Level: 4–5

Approximate Time Required: 20 minutes

Purpose: To provide experience in learning about language structure while creating a seasonal poem.

Materials: paper and pen or pencil
chalkboard

Structure and Conventions

Directions: Write the following words on the chalkboard: sunshine, thunder, lightning, sleet, tornado, drizzle, snowman, and raindrop. Students may suggest other words to add. Point out that these words are associated with weather.

Write the following poem on the chalkboard:

Blizzard

B lustery winds howl fiercely in the night.
L ights from candles flicker with the power gone.
I cy streets greet anyone foolish enough to drive.
Z ig-zagging snow whips every which way.
Z ippered in parkas, a few brave souls patrol.
A nxious faces press against cold panes of glass.
R oads disappear, hidden in drifts and blowing snow.
D angerous night to venture out in the storm.

Point out that the first letter of each word in each line of the poem read vertically spells the name of the poem. Each line in some way describes an aspect of the weather.

Each student is asked to choose one of the words from the chalkboard, another weather-related word, and compose one or more weather poems.

Allow time for students to share their poems aloud. The finished set might be bound in a classroom booklet of "Weather Poems" or put on a bulletin board.

՗Group Diamond Poem

Grade Level: 4–5

Approximate Time Required: 20 minutes

Purpose: To provide experience in learning about language structure while working as part of a group to create a shape poem.

Structure and Conventions

Materials: chalkboard

For each student:
a copy of A Diamond Poem reproducible on page 99
pen or pencil

Directions: Draw a large diamond shape on the chalkboard and tell students you are going to try to write a poem to fill this space. It will be a "diamond" poem. The poem will have seven lines. The first and last lines of the poem are words that in some way relate to each other but in other ways are very different from each other.

Allow time for students to select related-but-different words and put down these ideas on a section of the chalkboard. Possibilities include bud—blossom; brook—ocean; seed—pumpkin; baby—actress; page—novel; caterpillar—butterfly. Choose a promising pair of these words and place the words at the top and bottom of the empty diamond shape drawn on the chalkboard.

Hand out a copy of the Diamond Poem reproducible on page 99 to each student. Provide the rest of the instructions and work with the group to write the poem.

Line 1: One word which is the subject
Line 2: Two adjectives that describe the first word
Line 3: Three words ending in "ing" that describe the first word of the poem
Line 4: Four nouns. The first two relate to line 1, and the next two relate to line 7.
Line 5: Three words ending in "ing" that describe the last word of the poem
Line 6: Two adjectives that describe the last word of the poem
Line 7: One noun that is different from but related to line one

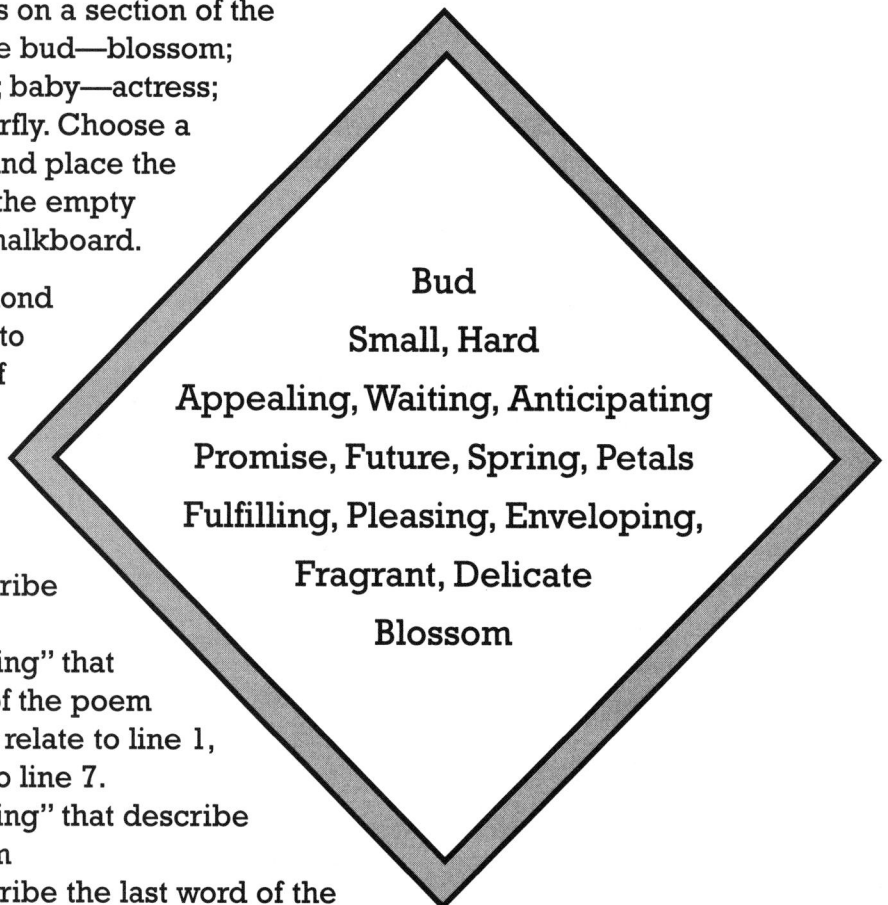

Bud

Small, Hard

Appealing, Waiting, Anticipating

Promise, Future, Spring, Petals

Fulfilling, Pleasing, Enveloping,

Fragrant, Delicate

Blossom

Name_____

A Diamond Poem

_____

_____

_____

_____

_____

_____

_____

The "Eyes" Have It

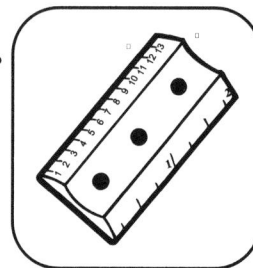

Grade Level: 4–5

Approximate Time Required: 20–30 minutes

Purpose: To provide experience in representing data in a bar graph.

Data Analysis

Materials: slips of paper to hand out to each student
chart paper or chalkboard
chalk

Directions: Hand out a slip of paper to each class member. Ask each person to write his or her name on the slip of paper. Then below their name they are to write:

> brown
> blue
> other

Ask each student to make an estimate of the following (without looking around the room at people's eyes) and to write their estimates on their piece of paper in the right categories:

> How many people in our classroom have brown eyes?
> How many people in our classroom have blue eyes?
> How many people in our classroom have eyes colored other than blue or brown?
> (gray, hazel, green)

On the back of the slip of paper, ask students to write and complete the following sentence: My own eye color is _____.
Collect the slips of paper.

Use a yardstick to make needed lines for a bar graph. Beneath the horizontal axis, write: brown, blue, other. Along the vertical axis write the numbers 1 to 20. Ask a student to read aloud the sentences about eye color while another student makes tally marks on the chalkboard. From a class of 30 students, you may have 18 students with brown eyes, 10 with blue eyes, and 2 with other (gray, hazel, green).

Ask two volunteers to construct the bar graph by filling in the data collected above for each eye color. Ask another two students to look over the "estimates." Did anyone estimate the correct number of brown, blue, and other eye colors of classmates? Who? If no one was exactly correct, who came closest?

A Peak Experience

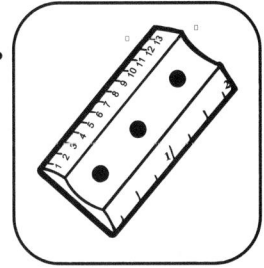

Grade Level: 4–5

Approximate Time Required: 20 minutes

Purpose: To provide experience in creating story problems.

Materials: chalkboard, mountain height data, paper and pencil

Directions: Share the information about mountains below with students either by writing it on the chalkboard, projecting it, or by running off multiple copies. Ask students to create three problems for classmates to solve. Allow time for the students to write out three problems and include the answers to the problems.

Collect the problems from students. Divide the class into six teams, Teams A, B, C, D, E, and F, with team members grouped together. Select and read a problem aloud. Ask each team to solve the problems as quickly as possible and hand in the right answer on a slip of paper. Keep a running score on the chalkboard. The first team to write down the correct answer and bring it up to you earns two points. The second team to come up with the right answer gets one point.

Highest Mountains by Continent

Mountain	Continent	Height (in feet)
McKinley	North America	20,320
Logan	North America	19,850
Popocatepetl	North America	18,696
Aconcagua	South America	22,834
Huascaran	South America	22,205
Chimborazo	South America	20,577
Everest	Asia	29,028
K2	Asia	28,250
Kanchenjunga	Asia	18,168
Kilimanjaro	Africa	19,340
Kenya	Africa	17,040
Margherita	Africa	16,821
Elbrus	Europe	18,468
Mont Blanc	Europe	15,781
Matterhorn	Europe	14,685

Prove It!

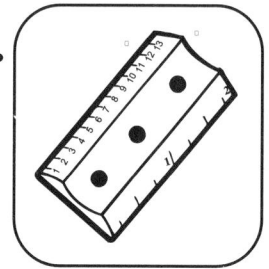

Grade Level: 4–5

Approximate Time Required: 15 minutes

Purpose: To provide experience in reasoning and problem solving using relationships and properties.

Materials: paper with two rectangles, each measuring 2 inches tall and 4 inches long scissors

Directions: Explain that students should cut the rectangles in a certain way by carefully following directions.

Demonstrate how to make the cut by taking one rectangle, making a single cut in it, which will yield two squares that are 2" x 2". Each student will then follow the example and cut the rectangle into two identical squares.

Cut the second rectangle, which is two inches tall and four inches long, into two pieces by making a cut from the bottom right corner to the top left corner, yielding two identical triangles.

Ask students to arrange all four pieces on their desks and to look at them carefully. The question they are to answer is: Does the triangle have the same area as the square? Discuss this. Most students will agree that they have the same area because halves of an equal area are equal to each other, but some may not be sure.

Ask if there is a way to prove that the triangle and the square have the same area. Let students try out their solutions. When individual students think they can prove this, ask for a volunteer to share his or her proof with the class. (In some cases, a student will simply put the square behind the triangle and cut off the piece that is not covered by the triangle. This cut-off piece will be exactly the right size to cover the remainder of the large triangle. See figure below.

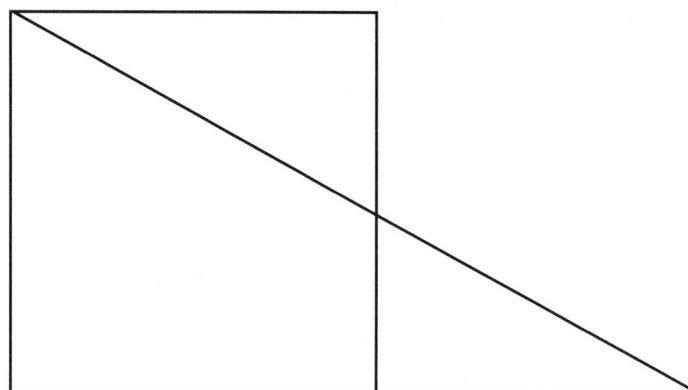

Lucky Seven

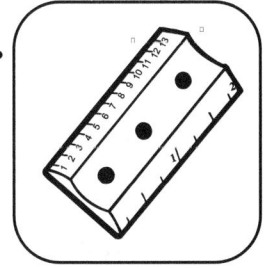

Grade Level: 4–5

Approximate Time Required: 20 minutes

Purpose: To provide experience in mathematical reasoning.

Materials: the sample problem below

Directions: Tell the class that you are thinking of a mystery number and have students try to guess that number by asking questions that can be answered "yes" or "no." They may have only seven tries, so they must come up with good questions that will make it possible to guess the mystery number.

As an example, tell students you are thinking of a mystery number that is between 1 and 100. A good question to narrow down the field might be, "Is the number bigger than 50?" If the answer is yes, half the possible numbers have been eliminated. If the answer is no, half the possible numbers have been eliminated. If the answer is yes, it is bigger than 50. A second good question might be, is it bigger than 75? This cuts the possible numbers in half again. If the answer to this question is no, you know that the mystery number is between 50 and 75. Knowing this much, a good question might be, "Is the number even?" If the answer is yes, half the possible remaining numbers have been eliminated. If the answer is no, half the possible numbers have been eliminated.

Suppose the mystery number is 60. You ask, "Is the number bigger than 50?" I answer yes. Then you ask, is it bigger than 75? I answer no. Then you ask, is the number even? I answer yes. You have used up three of your guesses, and you know that the number must be 52, 54, 56, 58, 60, 62, 64, 68, 70, 72, or 74. Write these numbers on the chalkboard. Remember you can ask only four more questions. What would be another good question to ask? Someone may come up with, is it smaller than 62? This eliminates half the numbers again. If the answer is yes, another question might be, is it smaller than 56? If the answer is no, you know that the mystery number must be 58 or 60, and you still have two guesses left!

Depending on the answers given, good questions might be "Is the mystery number evenly divisible by 5?" and "Are both digits in the numeral the same?"

Choose some random numbers and see how well the class does at guessing.

Symmetry

Grade Level: 4–5

Approximate Time Required: 20–30 minutes

Geometry

Purpose: To provide experience in working with symmetry

Materials: **For each student:**
pictures of people's faces cut from old magazines (different races and ages)
construction paper
glue
pencil
colored pencils
a copy of Finish the Faces reproducible on page 105

Directions: Talk to the class about lines of symmetry. Provide students with pictures of people's faces. Tell them that although human faces are not perfectly symmetrical, they are close to being symmetric. The faces should be cut in half vertically, down through the nose. There need to be enough pictures so that each student gets one-half of a face and some extras.

Pass the box containing the half faces around the room and allow each student to pick out a half-face. (There should be enough pictures in the box so that even the last student to pick still has some choices.)

Ask students to paste the selected half-face onto a sheet of drawing paper and then make the drawing "whole" by drawing in the missing half of the face. After sketching in the missing half, the student may use colored pencils to complete the drawing. Finished pictures might be mounted on a bulletin board.

Pass out copies of the reproducible Finish the Faces on page 105. Have students finish each face.

Finish the Faces

What's the Time?

Grade Level: 4–5

Approximate Time Required: 20 minutes

Purpose: To provide experience in working with 24-hour clocks.

Materials: pencil
paper

Number and Operations

Directions: Discuss different kinds of clocks with the class. Students may volunteer that they have a grandfather clock at home, that someone has a clock with Roman numerals on it, that some people have digital clocks, and that others have analog clocks. Some people may be familiar with atomic clocks.

Ask if students have seen a 24-hour clock. These are used by radio amateurs and some branches of government that use UTC, ZULU, or Greenwich time. The military uses a 24-hour clock, so that 3 o'clock in the afternoon is 1500 hours.

Write the times below on the chalkboard and ask students to convert them from a 24-hour clock to a 12-hour clock.

1. 1630

2. 0700

3. 2100

4. 1800

5. 2000

If there is time, a class discussion about telling time might also include the following topics:

Daylight Savings Time
Eastern Time
Central Time
Mountain Time
Pacific Time

Estimate Height of a Tree

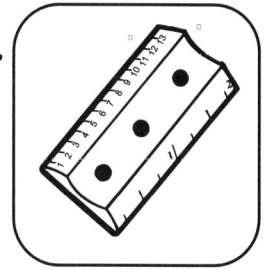

Grade Level: 4–5

Approximate Time Required: 20 minutes

Measurement

Purpose: To reinforce the concepts of measurement, proportion, and equations.

Materials: a yardstick

tape measures or meter sticks for each pair of students

a place on the playground where students can view a tree and its shadow

Directions: Ask students how they might measure a tall tree. Suggest that one way to measure a tree is to work a simple equation. To complete parts of the equation, students will need data obtained by measurement.

Have students each pick a partner and accurately measure and record on a 3" x 5" card the height of each partner. Then go outside on the playground to an area where a tree is casting a shadow. Have the partners measure the length of the tree shadow and record this information on their 3" x 5" card. Finally, have one partner measure the shadow of the other partner and record this information.

Come back inside and write the following equation on the chalkboard:

$$\frac{\text{height of tree}}{\text{length of tree shadow}} = \frac{\text{height of person}}{\text{length of person's shadow}}$$

Invite several persons to show their work on the chalkboard. Do most people get about the same estimate of the height of the tree? For those who do not come close to the answer that most students get, ask for suggestions as to what element in the equation might be wrong. Is there an obvious error in recording the height of the person? The length of the tree shadow? The length of the person's shadow?

Balloon Science

Grade Level: 4–5

Approximate Time Required: 30 minutes

Purpose: To learn more about air pressure.

Materials:
- a balloon
- a pop bottle
- a plastic glass
- a bucket of ice water
- a bucket of hot water
- a clock.

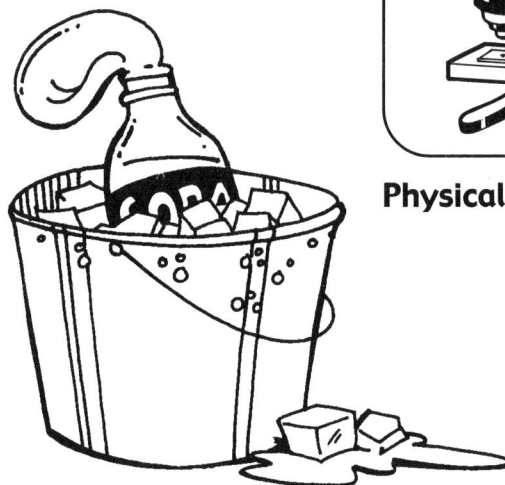

Physical Science

Directions: Tell students that they are going to observe two experiments using a balloon. Show the class a balloon and a clear plastic glass. Ask the class for suggestions on how to lift the glass without touching it with your hand. Listen to suggestions. Then explain one way to lift the glass using a balloon.

Dangle the balloon into the glass. Begin to blow up the balloon. The part of the balloon that is inside the glass will touch the sides of the glass as it inflates. By pinching the balloon closed to trap the air inside, you can lift the glass by holding the balloon. Discuss why this happens. (The air pressure inside the balloon exerted force outward in all directions.)

Now, take the balloon and fasten it over the neck of an empty pop bottle that is at room temperature. The bottle feels neither hot nor cold. Next put the bottle into a bucket of ice water. Note the time and wait fifteen minutes. Take the bottle out of the ice water. The bottle will feel cold.

Finally, put the cold pop bottle into a bucket of hot tap water and wait. The balloon will partially inflate. Note by the clock how long this takes to happen. Put the pop bottle back into the ice water. The balloon will deflate again. Note by the clock how long this takes to happen.

Discuss. When you put the bottle in hot water, you heated the air in the bottle. This caused the air molecules to spread out and take up more space, inflating the balloon in the process. When you put the balloon back into the ice water, the air cooled again. The cool air takes up less space, so the balloon deflates.

How High?

Grade Level: 4–5

Approximate Time Required: 20 minutes

Physical Science

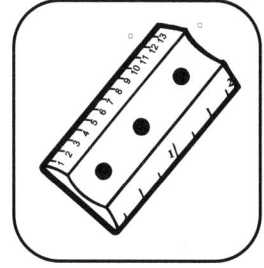

Data Analysis and Probability

Purpose: To provide experience working with the laws of gravity, predicting, observing, recording data, and graphing.

Materials: a large piece of oaktag
masking tape
several balls of different sizes
a yardstick
a chalkboard and chalk
a tape measure

Directions: Gather students in an area where they can watch a series of balls being dropped from the same height and measure the height of the ball bounce.

Prepare a graph either on a sheet of paper or on the chalkboard before students arrive. Across the horizontal bottom line of the graph are the names of the types of balls to be used: small rubber ball, basketball, golf ball, tennis ball, beach ball, etc. The vertical line of the graph will indicate inches, from one inch to forty-eight inches.

While showing the collection of balls of different sizes and materials, ask students if they can predict which of these balls will bounce highest. Allow time for discussion. Ask for a volunteer to hold a yardstick straight up and down. Ask for another student to hold a ball even with the top of the yardstick and drop it. Two "spotters" will indicate on the wall with a small piece of tape how high the ball bounced. Ask for another volunteer to drop the same ball and two more spotters to mark how high it bounced. Pick the average of the four spotters and use a tape measure to see how high the ball bounced. Ask a student volunteer to mark the level of the bounce on the graph.

Repeat this process with other volunteers dropping other balls and other "spotters" marking the height of the ball bounce.

Discuss the results of the experiment as shown on the graph. All the balls gained the same amount of energy from their fall. Then the downward force from gravity was converted into upward force to send the ball back into the air. Different materials and different sizes affect how high each will bounce.

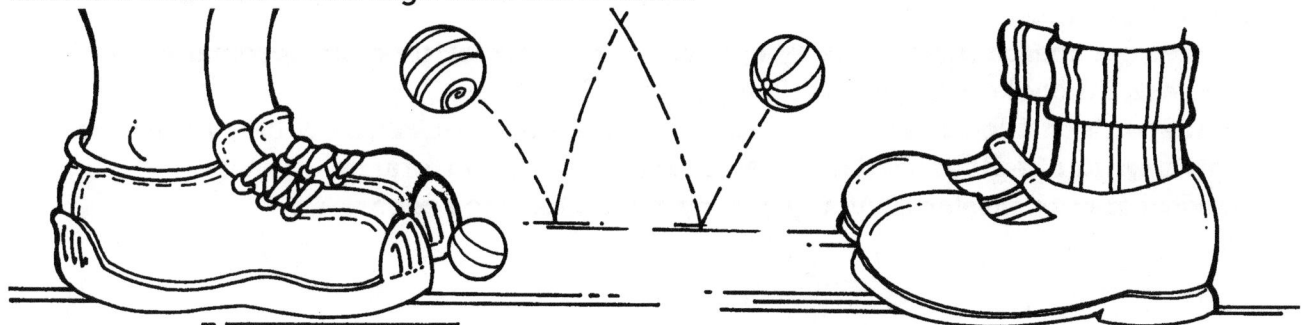

Edible Plants

Grade Level: 4–5

Approximate Time Required: 20 minutes

Life Science

Purpose: To provide experience in classification.

Materials: chalkboard   **For each student:**
pens
a copy of Edible Plants reproducible on page 111

Directions: Explain to students that they are going to work together to develop a chart of edible plants. Write the name of the chart, "Edible Plants" across the chalkboard. Underneath the title, place the subtitle of each of the columns. These subtitles are as follows:

**Roots   Stems   Bark   Leaves   Seeds   Flowers   Fruits with   Fruits without
                                                            Edible seeds   Edible seeds**

Have students complete their own charts using the reproducible on page 111. You may wish to have them work in groups. Lead a class discussion about fruits and vegetables that might be added to each column on the list. Some of these will be easy; others will be difficult. Students may ask why the word "vegetable" does not appear on the above list. Explain that botanists classify as "fruits" many of the fruits and vegetables that we eat. The "fruit" of the plant is the part that contains its seeds. So, using this definition, both a tomato and a squash are "fruits."

Call on volunteers to suggest items that can be added to the classification chart. When there is disagreement, ask the students who disagree to find a way to justify their answers. For example, if a student looks up "tomato" or "squash" in a standard dictionary it will discuss the "fruit" that people eat. When there is agreement, write the word in the correct column. Your finished list might contain the following:

Roots: beets, onions, potatoes, radishes, turnips, carrots, garlic, ginger
Stems: rhubarb, celery, asparagus
Bark: cinnamon
Leaves: lettuce, cabbage, parsley, spinach, kale, bay leaf, oregano, rosemary
Flowers: artichoke, saffron, cauliflower, broccoli
Fruits with edible seeds: banana, green beans, peas, squash, strawberry, tomatoes
Fruits without edible seeds: apple, cherry, peach, plum, orange
Seeds: caraway, mustard, nutmeg, poppy seeds, sesame seeds

Name _____

Edible Plants

Roots	Stems	Bark	Leaves	Seeds	Flowers	Fruits with Edible Seeds	Fruits without Edible Seeds

Friction

Grade Level: 4–5

Approximate Time Required: 20 minutes

Physical Science

Purpose: To demonstrate that surfaces rubbing against each other create friction and that friction slows thing down and creates heat.

Materials: a coffee can lid
a coffee can half-filled with sand
a thick piece of string
a sheet of waxed paper
a sheet of sand paper
a thermometer
some books

Directions: Explain to students that they will observe two experiments involving friction. Gather students in a position where they can clearly see the surface of a table. Tie a sturdy string about a lightweight book. Tie the other end of the string around a can of sand. Set the coffee can on its side on the table, dangle the book off the edge of the table, and see what happens. Depending on the weight of the book, the can may move toward the edge of the table or may not move.

Tape a sheet of smooth waxed paper on the table beneath the coffee can and repeat the experiment. Does the can move more easily? Discuss.

Tape a sheet of sandpaper beneath the coffee can and repeat the experiment. Does the can move less easily? Discuss.

(You may have to experiment with several objects until you have enough weight to pull the coffee can to the edge when it rests on a smooth surface. It will resist being moved when it rests on a rough surface.)

Now take the temperature of the sand that is in the coffee can and write this on the chalkboard. Keeping the lid on tightly, pass the can around to several student volunteers. Allow each student to vigorously shake the can of sand rapidly. Take the temperature of the sand again. Write the new temperature reading on the chalkboard. Did the temperature increase? Why? The sand particles rubbed against each other causing friction, and friction produces heat.

Inventions

Grade Level: 4–5

Approximate Time Required: 30–45 minutes

Purpose: To provide experience in identifying a simple problem, proposing a solution, evaluating a product or design, and communicating the design process to others.

Materials: paper
pencil

Directions: Suggest to students that each of us may have an idea for an invention that we think is needed and important although we may not know exactly how to build it. For this lesson, each student will come up with an idea for an invention that will provide a solution to a problem that many people commonly face in daily life. It may be an attempt to suggest a solution to a serious problem, or it may be humorous.

Explain to students that each proposed invention will be judged by the following criteria:

> - Does it address a real and significant problem?
>
> - Does it seem feasible?
>
> - Could it be produced at a reasonable price?
>
> - Would there be a demand for this product on the market?
>
> - Would this product be harmful to living things or the environment?

Each student should write a short paper on his/her invention in which the student gives the invention a name and tells what this invention does and why it is important. Include a drawing of the invention which may be realistic or fanciful.

Allow each student to present his or her invention before the class.

Then allow time for class evaluation of the invention using the criteria mentioned above.

Completed pages could be bound in a class book or displayed on a bulletin board.

Circling Butterflies

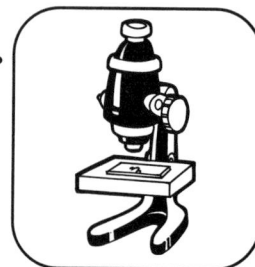

Grade Level: 4–5

Approximate Time Required: 20 minutes

Purpose: To provide experience with static electricity.

Materials: **For each pair of students:**
a comb
two feet of sewing thread
a square of tissue paper
scissors

Directions: Tell the class that they are going to work with partners and experiment with static electricity. One of the partners needs to have a pocket comb.

The partners will sit near each other. One will cut a butterfly from a small piece of tissue paper and will put two small holes in the body of the butterfly. The partner inserts a two-foot piece of sewing thread through the holes and ties the thread to the butterfly.

One partner will now hold the thread with the butterfly dangling from it while the partner runs a comb briskly through his or her hair for about two minutes. The partner then gently rubs the comb several times against the wings of the butterfly. (The tissue paper will probably be attracted toward the comb.)

The partner with the comb begins to comb his or her hair vigorously again. Then this partner takes the comb and holds it out close to, but not touching, the dangling butterfly.

The partners observe what happens to the butterfly. (It will move away from the comb.)

After all partners have been successful with this activity, discuss what happened.

What made the butterfly move? (static electricity)

Why is static created? (The friction of rubbing the comb through the hair causes the electrons to separate. The separated electrons collect on the comb.) In their own words students will explain that the charged comb carries extra electrons that carry an invisible electronic force.

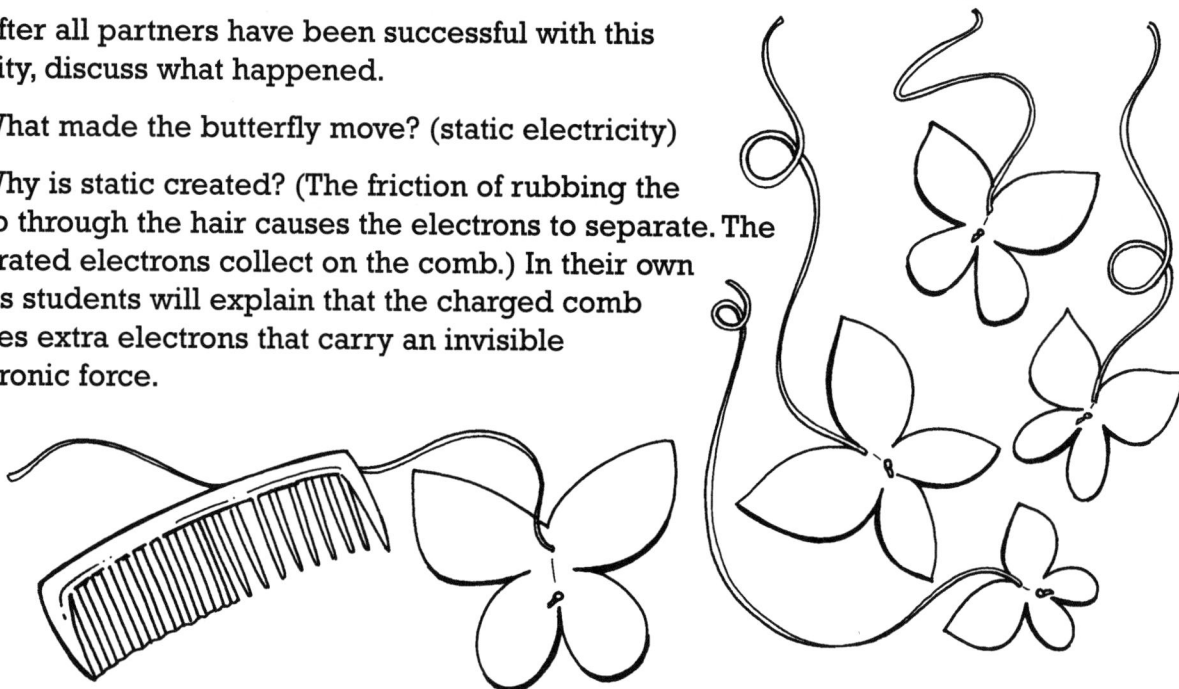

Surface Tension

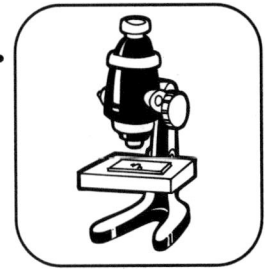

Grade Level: 4–5

Approximate Time Required: 20 minutes

Physical Science

Purpose: To learn about the surface tension of water.

Materials: a pan of water
piece of tissue
a needle
a bar of soap
a magnifying glass

Directions: Tell students that they will observe some demonstrations of surface tension. Gather the students around a table where they can easily observe what is going on.

Invite a student volunteer to take a needle and drop it point-end first into the pan of water. Students will observe that the needle sinks. Ask another student to lay the needle lengthwise on the water. It will still sink. Ask students if they can think of a way to put the needle in the water so that it will float on the surface. Listen to the various suggestions, and if appropriate, try them out.

Now take a piece of tissue paper about three inches square. Lay the needle flat on the piece of tissue. Ask for a volunteer to lay the tissue with the needle on it gently on the surface of the water. What happens? At first the tissue and the needle both float. As the tissue absorbs water, it sinks, but it leaves the needle still floating on the surface of the water.

Invite students to take turns looking at the floating needle with a magnifying glass. Ask what they observe. Students will report that they can see tiny dents around the needle. It is almost as if the water has a "skin."

Now ask students to observe carefully while a student takes a bar of soap and gently touches the top of the water with a bar of soap. The needle will soon sink.

Explain that at first the molecules of water at the surface were attracted to each other by surface tension. The force of the surface tension was greater than the force of gravity, so instead of sinking, the needle floated. But the soap interferes with the attraction that water molecules have for each other. The soap breaks the surface tension that was supporting the needle, and it sinks.

'Round the World Bingo

Grade Level: 4–5

Approximate Time Required: 10–20 minutes

Purpose: To increase global awareness and appreciate cultures and contributions of other countries of the world.

Materials: copies of the reproducible on page 117

Directions: Using the reproducible on page 117, students will move quietly around the classroom and fill in as many squares as possible. A student may use another student's name only once on the sheet. A student may score "'Round the World Bingo" when four squares down or across are filled in. At that time the student who called "'Round the World Bingo" will read out the names, and the student named will expand on the information. For example, if John has Mary's name written in the first box, John will call on Mary, and she will tell what foreign country she has visited. (If time permits, you may play longer and see if anyone can fill in the entire sheet.)

Name_____

has traveled to a foreign country _____	can read and write at least ten words in a foreign language _____	has a relative living in a foreign country _____	enjoys a music group from a foreign country _____
can name a sports star from a foreign country _____	has a family car that was made in a foreign country _____	ate in an ethnic restaurant sometime this month _____	can sing a song in a foreign language _____
lives in a home where more than one language is spoken _____	has a parent or close relative who was born in a foreign country _____	owns some foreign stamps or money _____	saw a TV program and learned something about a foreign country recently _____
can correctly give the name of a king, queen, prime minister, or other head of a foreign country _____	has had an overseas pen pal or has chatted online with a foreign-born person overseas _____	can cook a food dish from a foreign country _____	can name a foreign movie star and the name of one of his/her films _____

School Cheer

Grade Level: 4–5

Approximate Time Required: 20–30 minutes

Purpose: To explain how groups meet personal needs and promote the common good.

Materials: chalkboard
For each student:
paper
colored pencils or markers
a copy of the Pennants reproducible on page 119

Individuals, Groups & Institutions

Directions: Discuss with the class how although each individual keeps his or her personal identity, individuals join many different sorts of groups. Ask students to identify some of the groups to which they belong. Write those that are suggested on the chalkboard. These might include the following:

Family	School Newspaper Club
Class	School Newspaper Club
School	Drama Club
Scout Group	Basketball Team
Church Group	State
Summer Camp	Nation
Little League	School Band, Choir, or Orchestra

Many groups have a song or cheer which helps cement the identity of the group. Use the cheer at the bottom of this page as an example. Ask students to work in teams of three or four to make up a new school cheer. At the end of the class work period, ask each team to come up front and give the cheer to the class.

(Sample)
Bear Creek, Bear Creek is our name!
Victory, victory, we will claim!
Are we winners? Well, I guess!
Bear Creek, Bear Creek! Yes, yes. yes!

Hand out copies of the Pennants reproducible. Have each student create a pennant for their school and one for any other favorite team.

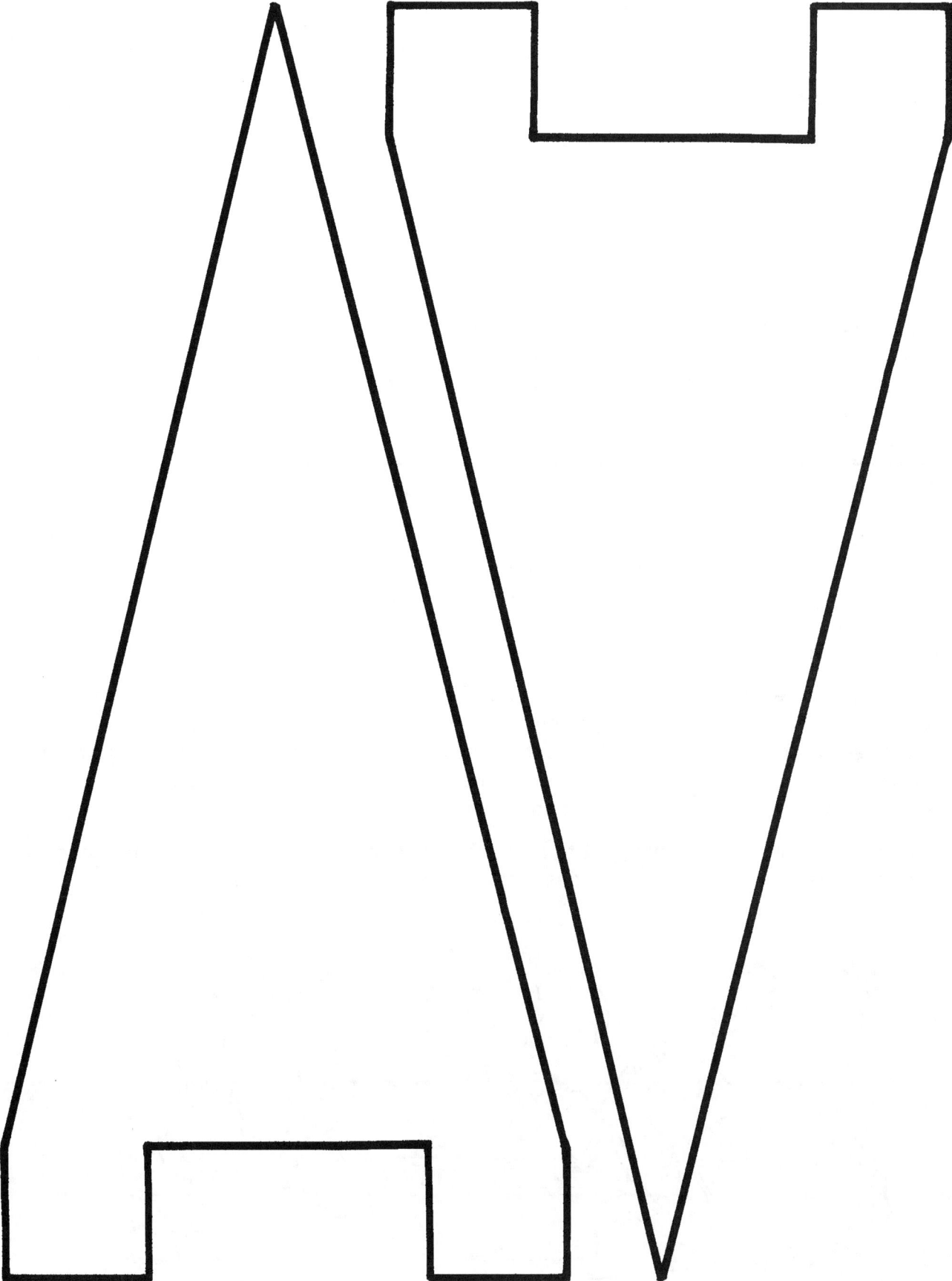

Pennants

© Carson-Dellosa

CD-0048 *The Substitute's Own Survival Guide*

The Cornerstone

Grade Level: 4–5

Approximate Time Required: 20–30 minutes

Purpose: To provide an opportunity to identify possible cultural and community changes over time.

Time, Continuity, and Change

Materials: paper
pen or pencil

Directions: Set the scene for this assignment by pointing out that it has been common when an important building is erected to include in a cornerstone certain items that were in some way important to the people living in that place at that particular time. Then at some future date, when perhaps the building is being torn down to make way for some new project, the old cornerstone acts like a time capsule, revealing what people were thinking and talking about and what they considered important fifty or a hundred years ago.

When, for example, the state capitol building cornerstone was laid on the Fourth of July in Denver, Colorado, in 1890, the following were some of the items that were placed in a copper box in the huge cornerstone: a copy of the Colorado and federal constitution, a Holy Bible, an American flag, a city directory, a map of the state, some gold coins, and copies of several local newspapers.

Have students imagine a new and big building is going to be built in their town, and they are part of the committee of people to decide what items should be placed in the cornerstone. Have them each make a list of five to ten fairly small items that they would suggest should be included in the cornerstone, and for each one, write a few sentences explaining why this item is important and should be included.

If time permits, allow volunteers to share their lists and their reasons for including the items. Are there certain common ideas that most people have suggested?

Imaginary Islands

Grade Level: 4–5

Approximate Time Required: 30 minutes

Space and Place

Purpose: To provide experience in preparing a map legend and to demonstrate an understanding of the relationship between physical features, natural resources, and land use.

Materials: drawing paper
pencil
colored pencils
classroom map of the United States or of the world

Directions: Use one or more classroom maps to point out that major cities tend to develop along ports, rivers, and railroad lines. Discuss the reasons for this in terms of power and the production and distribution of goods.

Discuss the symbols that are used on the map legend. The map or maps you are using in the classroom may use different size print to designate the population of cities, have a star for state capitals, or rivers in blue, etc. What types of markings are used to designate state or country boundaries?

Ask each student to create on his or her piece of paper an original map of an imaginary island. Students are to design the shape of the island and name it. On the map they should locate major cities, put in railroads and highways, have agricultural and industrial areas, and whatever else is of interest.

Stress that each map needs to have a legend with symbols and that these symbols should appear in correct locations on the map.

Tape the maps up on the board and ask for volunteers to describe these new islands, to point out where they would be located in the world in terms of longitude and latitude, what the climate might be like on the island, what kinds of flora and fauna might be found there, and where major political and geographical features are located.

Mapping the Neighborhood

Grade Level: 4–5

Approximate Time Required: 20–30 minutes

Purpose: To identify institutions that promote the common good.

Materials: white paper
               pen
               pencil
               colored pencils or markers
               chalkboard

Individuals, Groups & Institutions

Space and Place

Directions: Discuss with the class the important things, places, and buildings that communities have to serve the needs of people who live in them. As students brainstorm and volunteer ideas, write them on the chalkboard: The following list might be generated:

> **Parks**
> **Recreation Centers**
> **Ball Fields, Stadiums**
> **Schools**
> **Libraries**
> **Churches**
> **City Offices**
> **Shopping Center and Stores**
> **Banks, Service Stations,**
> **Restaurants**
> **Hospitals**
> **Post Office**
> **Police Station, Justice Center**
> **Fire Houses**

After the list is created, ask students to volunteer to come up and draw a symbol next to each to represent that type of service. (For example, a cross might indicate a church, and a bell might indicate a school.)

Then ask students to make a drawing of their neighborhood and try to place the symbols for the institutions listed above that exist in their part of town in roughly the right location. Students might want to include major streets. If time permits, share these neighborhood maps or display them on a bulletin board.

Time Line

Grade Level: 4–5

Approximate Time Required: 20–30 minutes

Time

Purpose: To provide experience in constructing a time line of events in American history.

Materials: masking tape
chalkboard

For each pair of students:
10 index cards (3" x 5") or slips of paper

For each student:
a copy of My Time Line reproducible on page 124

Directions: Ask each person to choose a partner. Have students arrange themselves so they are sitting next to their partners. Write the following events on the chalkboard and gives each pair of students ten 3" x 5" cards or slips of paper, on which to write the following events, one to a card.

---

1. **Early Anasazi Cliff-Dwelling Society**
2. **Attack on Pearl Harbor**
3. **Beginning of Civil War**
4. **Pilgrims Celebrating the First Thanksgiving**
5. **Signing of Declaration of Independence**
6. **Lewis and Clark Expedition**
7. **Completion of Transcontinental Railroad**
8. **California Gold Rush**
9. **Louisiana Purchase**
10. **DeSoto's Exploration in Florida**

Ask students to use whatever resources are available in the classroom (texts, computers, reference books) to locate the date of each of the ten events, write it on the card or slip of paper, and arrange the cards in a stack, with the most recent event on top. Then draw a time line on the chalkboard beginning with 1000 and going up to the present time. Ask for volunteers from the pairs of students to come up and write the date and add one of their cards to the time line, using a piece of masking tape to hold the card in place.

Discuss the time line. Does anyone challenge any of the dates indicated or the order of events? If time permits, add to the time line other dates of events of interest to the students such as the September 11, 2002, terrorist attack.

Using the My Time Line reproducible on page 124, have students make up time lines of their own lives. Have them draw pictures in the boxes of events from their lives.

Name_____

My Time Line

Where in the World?

Grade Level: 4–5

Approximate Time Required: 20–30 minutes

Purpose: To discuss how people produce, distribute, and consume goods.

Materials: chalkboard

Directions: Lead a brainstorming session and note ideas on the chalkboard.

In the United States, we grow and make goods that are sold to people in other countries of the world. In return, the produce and products of other countries are bought in the United States and used by many of us.

Is anyone wearing or does anyone have in his or her desk or backpack something that was made in another country? What is it? (Record these responses on a section of the chalkboard. Students may identify shoes made in China, a shirt made in India, a T-shirt that was made in Mexico.)

Enlarge the area of interest by asking, do any of you have items in your home or your garages that were made in another country? Record responses on a section of the chalkboard. (Students may identify a car made in Germany, a microwave made in Korea, a toaster made in China, etc.) Ask if there are items in the grocery store in the produce section that come from other countries. (Identify these on the chalkboard.)

Ask students to discuss what items made in the United States are sent to other countries. Record these on another section of the chalkboard. Students might suggest cars, wheat, videos, etc.

As time and interest permit, discuss natural resources, labor, supply and demand, and how the market determines the goods and services that are to be produced and distributed, and the role that prices, incentives, and profits play in competitive market systems.

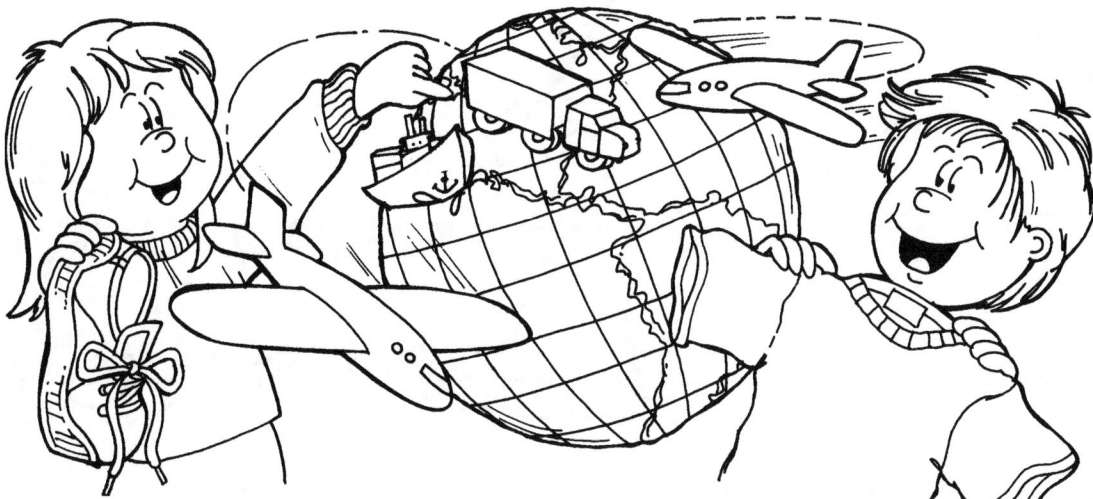

Awards

I was Helpful!

Presented to _____

by _____

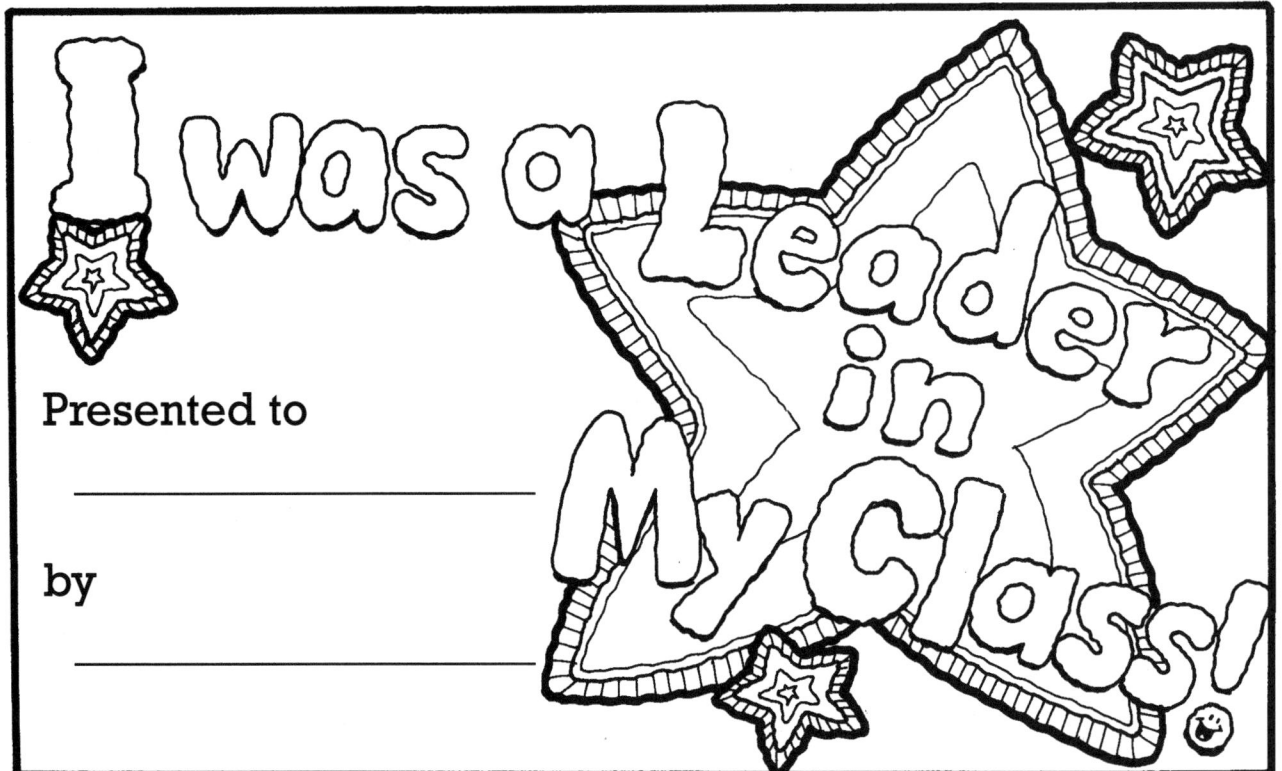

I was a Leader in My Class!

Presented to

_____

by

_____

I was polite and respectful!

Presented to _____

by _____

I was GREAT

when my teacher was absent!

Presented to

_____

by

_____

Answer Key

Page 21
1. 6 cars
2. 72 cookies
3. 21 books

Page 25
1. 8   Child illustrates 3 + 5 = 8
2. 10   Child illustrates 3 + 2 + 5 = 10
3. 8   Child illustrates 2 + 4 + 2 = 8
4. 11   Child illustrates 8 + 1 + 2 = 11
5. 9   Child illustrates 10 - 1 = 9
6. 10   Child illustrates 3 + 2 + 5 = 10

Page 39
1. Color everything but the thong and shorts.
2. Color the visor, swimsuit, trunks, sandal, and hat.
   (Some students may include the T-shirt.)
3. Color the rain hat, boot, raincoat, and umbrella.
   (Students might color shorts, swimsuit, or thong. Ask them to defend their answers.)
4. Color socks, glove, long pants, sweater, shoe, and scarf.

Page 49
The plane and balloon should be pasted on the sky.
The boat and canoe should be pasted on the water.
The car and truck should be pasted on the highway.

Page 62
1. 1 penny, 0 nickels, 1 dime, and 1 quarter.
2. 2 pennies, 5 nickels, 0 dimes, and 0 quarters.
3. 1 penny, 0 nickels, 10 dimes, and 0 quarters.
4. 0 pennies, 3 nickels, 1 dime, and 0 quarters.
5. 0 pennies, 0 nickels, 2 dimes, and 2 quarters.
6. 0 pennies, 20 nickels, 0 dimes, and 0 quarters.
7. 5 pennies, 0 nickels, 0 dimes, and 1 quarter.
8. 0 pennies, 0 nickels, 0 dimes, and 8 quarters.
9. 0 pennies, 10 nickels, 0 dimes, and 0 quarters.
10. 1 penny, 0 nickels, 3 dimes, and 1 quarter.

Page 67
1. No   3. Yes
2. No   4. No

Page 69
1. 3, 6, 9, 12, 15, 18, 21, 24, 27, 30, 33, 36, 39, 42, 45, 48, 51, 54, 57, 60, 63, 66, 69, 72, 75, 78, 81, 84, 87, 90, 93, 96, 99
2. 5, 10, 15, 20, 25, 30, 35, 40, 45, 50, 55, 60, 65, 70, 75, 80, 85, 90, 95, 100
3. 15, 30, 45, 60, 75, 90

Page 70
1. No   3. No
2. Yes   4. No
         5. Yes

Page 83

Page 106
1. 4:30 p.m.
2. 7:00 a.m.
3. 9:00 p.m.
4. 6:00 pm.
5. 8:00 p.m.

Page 123
1. Between 1000 and 1300
2. 1941
3. 1861
4. 1621
5. 1776
6. 1804–1806
7. 1869
8. 1849
9. 1803
10. 1539–1542